Possessing Your Pleasant Mountains

DIVAS MAKONI

authorHOUSE®

AuthorHouse™ UK
1663 Liberty Drive
Bloomington, IN 47403 USA
www.authorhouse.co.uk
Phone: UK TFN: 0800 0148641 (Toll Free inside the UK)
*   UK Local: (02) 0369 56322 (+44 20 3695 6322 from outside the UK)*

Published by AuthorHouse 05/01/2018

ISBN: 978-1-5462-9221-0 (sc)
ISBN: 978-1-5462-9220-3 (e)

DEDICATION

I take pleasure in dedicating possessing your Pleasant Mountains to all the parents and all teenagers throughout the world. There are pleasant mountains for you to possess.

Love you,

Divas Makoni

INTRODUCTION

But the children of Joseph said, "The mountain country is not enough for us; and all the Canaanites who dwell in the land of the valley have chariots of iron, both those who are of Beth Shean and its towns and those who are of the Valley of Jezreel".

Joshua 17:16

God gave me this scripture as a message to our local church which became the foundation of this book. I have come to realize that many people live their lives murmuring and complaining. They live mediocre lives without fulfilling their destiny. They fail to see the good things that God has blessed them with. God has given them treasure which is still locked up on the inside. These treasures include books, films, poetry, businesses, gifts and inventions. They do not see that indeed God has blessed them. All they do is to mourn and complain when God wants them to possess their pleasant mountains and enjoy the hidden treasure.

At one time, I was one of those people. I am so glad God gave me this scripture which opened my life. I now see life differently. I will look for the positives in any situation. Now I want everyone else to have the same attitude. I want them to clear their woods so as to possess their pleasant mountains.

God has already made plans and provisions to bless his children. How can God's plans become real in your life? Read on, and remember God loves you. He is a good God and His love endures forever. He wants you to clear your woods so as to possess your pleasant mountains!

CHAPTER 1

GOD'S PROMISE

Then God blessed them, and God said to them, "Be fruitful and multiply; fill the earth and subdue it; have dominion over the fish of the sea, over the birds of the air, and over every living thing that moves on the earth".

Genesis 1:28

In the beginning God created man in His own image. God called the man Adam. Adam was blessed by God. The blessing that Adam received enabled him to be fruitful and to succeed in whatever project that he would embark on. This blessing also enabled Adam to have dominion over all of God's creation. The blessing that Adam received applies to all humanity as he was the first man that ever lived. All the people came through him. They also received the same blessing as Adam. This means that you have been born blessed. When God created you, He spoke a blessing over your life. He made you to be fruitful and you were given dominion. You have the same blessing as it was given to Adam.

The lord has prepared everything that you will ever need. He has put all that you will need in life at a specific location for you to go in and possess so as to enjoy life. This specific location is what I call your pleasant mountains. You need to utilise what has been provided for you in your pleasant mountains so as to live a life of abundance. What you ever need is found in your pleasant mountains.

It has been God's plan for you to live in prosperity. God wants you to live a life of increase. The Lord wants to show you how to prosper so that you live a life of abundance. He wants to see His children succeed in business, academics, sports and politics and many other fields. You have been created to have businesses exploiting the marine, land and air resources as He said you have to dominate the sea, air and the land. You have been designed to benefit from the resources that God put in your pleasant mountains.

You are blessed with the spirit of multiplication. Success is not determined by your background, status, gender or education. True success is in found in your pleasant mountains. Therefore your success is guaranteed as long as you possess your pleasant mountains. You have the ability to possess these pleasant mountains. The pleasant mountains have been prepared for you by the Lord. Always remember that you are a winner who has been born to dominate natural resources.

You have been given dominion over the fish of the sea. Fish is a symbol of abundance. You were never meant to lack or struggle in life. Lack or poverty is an evil spirit which seeks to cause misery and bring doubt in your mind. It tries to portray God as a father who cannot provide for your needs as His child. Many Christians today believe that it is alright to suffer on earth. They believe that this is the will of God for them. Many wait for abundance in heaven not on this earth. This is the deception of the devil, which is an error to be corrected by today's church.

Genesis 1:28 describes what the spirit of man carries. It carries fruitfulness, ability to multiply and domination of natural resources. The physical man was later formed out of the ground. Therefore the physical is supposed to benefit from the blessing that spirit of man has. The children of God need to understand what they have been empowered to do by the Lord almighty. Such an understanding will make you to succeed in life.

You can only succeed if you discover the blessing of God upon your spirit. He has given you a spirit of multiplication. You cannot remain in the same position year after year. There ought to be visible progress in your life. You have been enabled to enjoy the fruit of your labour. You have to take control of your pleasant mountains. You ought to benefit from what the oceans, land and air offers.

Enjoy the gold, bdellium, onyx stone, diamond, oil found in both the land and oceans. You have been empowered to have projects in mining, fishing, forestry, agriculture, aviation and many other areas. In all these projects you are assured of profit and increase. The Lord has made a promise which shall not be broken. He stands to fulfil what He has promised to you.

The promise

And the Lord appeared unto Abram, and said; to your descendants I will give this land.

Genesis 12:7

God promised to give Abraham and his descendants a land that had beautiful cities, houses already built, wells, vineyards and olive trees. This land had beautiful cities full of good things. The children of Israel would also find vineyards and Olive trees in the Promised Land. The also had brooks of water which flowed out of fountains and the hills. In other words God gave the children of Israel more than they could ever wish for. The

Lord had prepared all the good things for them long before they were born. *So I have come down to deliver them out of the land of the Egyptians, and to bring them up from the land to a good land, to a land flowing with milk and honey, to the place of the Canaanites and the Hittites and the Amorites and the Perizzites and the Hivites and the Jebusites.*

Exodus 3:8

The Lord promised them good land in Canaan. It was different from the land of Egypt where they got water from the Nile River. This land received rainwater which quite different from the land of Egypt where they used water from the rivers. The children of Israel would not be limited by natural weather conditions. The other advantage of the land in Canaan was the availability of fertile soils. Fertile soils would enable the children of Israel to grow Wheat and Barley and other crops. It was therefore a land of abundance. This was in line with prophecy as God had promised them that they would lack nothing. The land was also rich in minerals. The children of Israel would also have lucrative mining projects.

Deuteronomy 8:7-9

God promised to give Abraham and his descendants a good land. This was a land of abundance. The land was rich minerals such as Iron and Copper. The children of Israel would have abundant foodstuffs such as wheat, barley and bread. The land also had vines, fig trees, pomegranates, olive oil, and honey in the hills and valleys. There were also beautiful cities already built that the children of Israel would dwell in.

God has a place where he is going to give you houses, businesses, minerals, arable land, livestock and food. He is ready to show you that place so that you can go in and possess it. He also wants to take you to a place where your gifts and talents will blossom and your greatness would be revealed. He has a geographical area where you can be actors in that movie, a place where you can play any sport or where people can embrace your fashion designs. He has prepared you for take over. It's time for you to possess your pleasant mountains.

God mentioned that this land was already inhabited. It was inhabited by Canaanites, Hittites, Amorites, Perizzites and Hivites. This seemed to be a huge setback for the children of Israel. But God promised the children of Israel ownership of the land of Canaan from the time of Abraham. The Lord gave them the land before they were born. All they had to do was to go in and possess the land regardless of the presence of the enemies. The Lord had empowered them to take over the land. They had to fight for their inheritance. God had already given them victory over the Canaanites with their iron chariots. The promise of milk and honey was a sign that God had given them victory. He gave the land to Abraham even before he had a son. Likewise God has prepared good things for you even before your birth. This shows that our Lord is a God of provision. He wants you to live in abundance. This is a sign of His unfailing love for you.

The Lord almighty has prepared wonderful things for you as His child. He loves you. The Lord thinks about you all the time. He gave you a crown of glory, honour and dominion. God has given you dominion over all His creation. That is why He always thinks about you. I know that you were never meant to suffer in this world. God is mindful of your needs. He thinks about you all the time. He loves you. He has already prepared for you to prosper. *He says for I know the plans I have for you…plans to prosper you, to give you a future and a hope.*

Jeremiah 29:11

When you go through challenges you need to understand that God has a way out. He has an exit route for you to take. All you need to do is to believe in him. He is faithful. Once he makes a promise he will surely fulfil it. He stands ready to see His plans becoming a reality in your life. These plans shall become real when you possess your pleasant mountains. Do not doubt God. Just believe and you shall see good things coming to you.

He promised Israel a land flowing with milk and honey to their father Abraham centuries before they inherited the land. He promised to give you your pleasant mountains. God planned for your life even before the foundation of the ages. He says to Jeremiah, *"Before I formed you in the womb I knew you"*.

Jeremiah 1:5

He has already prepared good things for your enjoyment before you were born. You will succeed in life because everything has been made ready for you. All that you need is adequate preparation in order to receive.

The promise to the children of Joseph

Joseph was the eleventh son of Jacob. Jacob was a grandson of a man called Abraham. He became the owner of the land of Canaan when God gave the land to Abraham. This Joseph lived in Egypt for most of his adult life. He went to Egypt after a series of unfortunate events. He was rejected by his jealous brothers who sold him to traders who were going to Egypt. This was done as a form of revenge for thr preferential treatment that Joseph received from his father. His brothers thought that this was the demise of Joseph. However God orchestrated the whole programme.

Joseph got married and had two sons while he was in Egypt. The first one was called Manasseh. The second one was called Ephraim. When his father Jacob saw the two boys he blessed them and declared that these two were to be treated like his own biological sons. This meant that Joseph's two sons were also given land in the land of Canaan like their uncles. So when Israel was inheriting the land these two got land as the tribes of Joseph.

These two boys were born in Egypt which was a land of bondage. They did not have any right to inherit land in Egypt. They never imagined themselves owning property. However this changed one day when their father took them to see their sick grandfather. This visit changed their lives forever. They were told that God had promised to give them land in Canaan. They could not believe what they were hearing from grandpa. So they were landowners just like other Egyptian children. Within the twinkling of an eye their lives changed forever. This shows us that the life of a child of God is not determined by what they pass through but by what God has already made available through Jesus Christ.

Your current problems are not your identity. You are not destined to a life of lack, suffering and regret. Any situation you might find yourself in is temporal. It is subject to change. Ephraim and Manasseh grew up without family. They did not have cousins and nephews like other children in their neighbourhood. They did not know that there were mountains which had their names. These mountains were later to be named mountains of Ephraim.

The Lord has prepared good things for you long before you were born. There is a property with your name on it. There are companies with your name waiting for you to take over. You are bon blessed just like Ephraim and Manasseh. You need to ask the Lord where your pleasant mountains are. Go in and possess them and enjoy the life that God has prepared for you. God has given you property with your name. No one can change that.

The pleasant mountains

God had already made available mountains for the children of Joseph long before they were born. The land that God had promised to their forefathers was described by Moses, the servant of God as the "pleasant mountains"... *the good land beyond the Jordan, those pleasant mountains.*

Deuteronomy 4:25

It was a land of lush hills, valleys and mountains. Indeed it was a land of milk and honey. The two boys must have been overjoyed. So the God of their fathers loved them too. So they were not second class citizens not entitled to any property. They could not wait to inherit their land in the pleasant mountains.

But the land which you cross over to possess is a land of hills and valleys, which drinks water from the rain of heaven, a land for which the Lord your God cares, the eyes of the Lord your God are always on it, from the beginning of the year to the very end of the year.

Deuteronomy 11:11-12

The pleasant mountains were also given to the children of Joseph through a prophetic word. These mountains were described as the everlasting hills. This was a place where the blessing that belonged to Joseph was located. It was a land of abundance and overflow. The inheritance that the sons of Joseph were to possess would belong to them forever.

Joseph is a fruitful bough,

…his braches run over the wall,

The blessing of your father have excelled the blessings of my ancestors,

*Up to the utmost bound of the **everlasting hills***

Genesis 49: 22-26

This shows that you can go around thinking that you are useless when in fact you are an important person in the eyes of the Lord. All you need is to find out what God has prepared for you. He has prepared good things for everyone. Your success is determined by what God has already promised. The moment you shall find out that you own properties, gold mines, fashion range, movies, television stations and your life will change. What the world considers useless is valuable in the eyes of God. Do not commit suicide because you are heavy in debt. Ask God to reveal what He has prepared for you. You might be shocked that you have oil underneath your shack. Ask Ruth the widow who could not even afford a meal who became the co-owner of Boaz Estates (Pty) LTD in one day!

CHAPTER 2

PLACE OF POSSESSION

... Get out of your country to a land that I will show you.

Genesis 12:1

There is a place where you belong and a place where you do not belong. There are things in life that require you to move from where you are staying to another place. This concept is clearly demonstrated in the lives of Elijah and Abraham. God instructed Abraham and Elijah to leave the places that they were currently staying. He had already given them the place where they were supposed to go. This demonstrates that your blessing is tied to a specific geographical area. You need to identify the area where your blessing is located. All you need to do is to find the area and go in to possess your pleasant mountains.

9

God told Abraham that he did not belong to the land called Haran. He had to move out of that place for God to bless him. God's blessing for Abraham was tied to the land of Canaan. Therefore Abraham did not belong to Haran. He had to move to Canaan. Canaan was a land which was chosen by God for him and also his descendants. His descendants would be blessed in Haran, a place that God had decided to give them.

This shows that your blessings are found in your own Canaan. Do not remain in Haran but find your Canaan where your blessings are. God has prepared your Canaan before you were born. You will be surprised to find out how your life will change as soon as you discover your Canaan. Change your location and heaven will open for you. Even though you are in the world you are not of this world. He has already blessed you with every spiritual blessing in the heavenly places (Ephesians 1:3). These blessings are meant to manifest in your physical life. God blesses you when you get to the place where He wants you to be. You can only excel when you get to the place prepared for you by God. So you do not belong to all places. Your breakthrough is at the right place assigned to you by God. God has prepared a place for you to prosper. THIS IS where you will live in abundance and in peace.

The children of Israel were the descendants of Abraham. Abraham was the father of Isaac. Isaac was the father of Jacob. Jacob's name was also changed by God. It was changed to Israel. The children of Israel belonged to a place that had been prepared for them by God in Canaan. The blessing for sons of Joseph, Ephraim and Manasseh were tied to the pleasant mountains in the land of Canaan not in Egypt were they were born. This is also shows you that you can remain in Egypt without any property. You only get property when you get to the land of Canaan.

You can live a life of toil and lack because they are in the wrong place. Your breakthrough is in another place. Identify the place where you can possess your pleasant mountains. Your lack is artificial and temporary. All you need to do is to change your position. Go the place that has been given to you by the Lord. God gave the children of Israel land and cities which they had not worked for. *I have given you a land for which you did not labour, and cities which you did not build…*

Joshua 24:13

All they needed to do was to follow God's instruction to leave Egypt for Canaan where they could possess their pleasant mountains in the Promised Land. You have to find the land which has your name on it. Do not try to work hard in the wrong place. Find the land of your breakthrough and enjoy what God has assigned for you. That is the reason why He instructed Moses to deliver the children of Israel out of the land of Egypt and take them to Canaan so as to inherit their pleasant mountains.

The Lord gave similar instructions to Prophet Elijah. He was told to go to the brook Cherith where he would get water during a time of a famine. It was at this place where God commanded Ravens to feed the prophet of God. There is a place where God has already orchestrated for your gift to bloom. There is a team where you shall play and shine. As long as you are not in that team you can play but you will be limited. Sometimes the coach will not accept your gift. But as soon as join the team that God said you shall play for you start to excel.

Get away from here and turn eastward, and hide by the Brook Cherith, which flows into the Jordan.

1 Kings 17:3

At times God changes the place with time. God did the same thing with Elijah. After some time the brook dried. It looked like this marked the end of God's supply, but God had another plan in His divine plan. He told the prophet to change location. His place of provision had changed. He had to go to a place called Zarephath. Now he was going to be fed not by a raven but by a widow. God did not provide a rich couple to feed Elijah but a poor widow who had her last meal before dying. God's ways are not our ways. He did not choose a rich businessman but a poor widow. He wants you to understand that it is not about what we you see with your physical eyes but what God has in the spirit.

Arise, go to Zarephath, which belongs to sidon, and dwell there.

1 Kings 17:9

Provision

Provision is a confirmation that you are in the right place. To show that Abraham's descendants were now in the right place God provided for them. He provided milk and honey, fruits, cities and land. God multiplied Abraham when he got to the Promised Land. This was the place where God had decided to bless him. The Lord gave him Isaac as a sign that he was now in the right place. God's provision was tied to the land of Canaan. God's promises are unveiled when you get to the place where He wants you to go. He is a God of increase. *Then I took your father Abraham from the other side of the river, led him throughout the land of Canaan, and multiplied his descendants and gave him Isaac.*

Joshua 24:3

I have given you a land for which you did not labour and cities which you did not build and you dwell in them. You eat of the vineyards and olive groves which you did not plant.

Joshua 24:13

The Lord also demonstrated the same principle to Elijah. He told him to go to the Brook of Cherith. The brook would provide water to him to drink. This brook was a tributary of the Jordan River whose waters were dirty and so not good enough for human consumption. So the tributary would be a source of clean drinking water for him. The Lord also provided the ravens to feed him there. The ravens gave him bread and water as a sign that he was in the right place.

However this place was a temporal arrangement. God instructed Elijah to move to another place. He told him to go a place called Zarephath. The Lord also provided food for him through a widow. This shows you that your blessings are in the pleasant mountains. You might complain that there is nothing good in these mountains. But what you consider useless is what the Lord can use to bless you. Elijah's sustenance was in a widow not a rich businessman. Therefore you ought to possess these pleasant mountains where your provision has been placed by the Lord.

And it will be that you shall drink from the brook, I have commanded the ravens to feed you there. The ravens brought him bread and meat in the morning, and bread and meat in the evening; and he drank from the brook.

1 Kings 17:4, 6

I have commanded a widow there to provide for you.

1 Kings 17: 9

Property in the Canaanite hills

According to the South African Oxford School Dictionary, the term property refers to a building or someone's land. In Joshua 17 v 18 Joshua gave the children of Joseph property in the mountains of Ephraim. They could even extend their property by cutting the woods. They could extend their property like branches over the wall as it had been prophesied by their father Israel. The children of Joseph had to possess these pleasant mountains in order to receive what the Lord had promised them through their fathers.

*But the **mountain country** shall be yours. Although it is wooded, you shall cut it down, and its farthest extent shall be yours.*

Joshua 17:18

The Lord Almighty wants you to own properties. God gave property to Abraham, Isaac, Jacob and Israel. He gave him land for himself and his descendants as a permanent inheritance. The Lord has prepared a mountain that he wants you to inherit. He has already empowered you to inherit the property. The mountain can be a physical or a spiritual place. The mountain can be an innovation, a book, a movie, a farm, buildings, a business, or ministry. You need to identify what God has put in you and then focus on that god given ability so as to enjoy a better life.

*And the Lord said to Abram, after lot had separated from him: Lift your eyes now and look from the place where you are are-northward, southward, eastward and westward; for all the **land** which you see I give to you and your descendants forever.*

Genesis 13:4-16

God kept his promise to Abram. He also gave property to Isaac. God told Isaac not to move out of the place where he was staying. God promised to bless him in the land. God gave him property in the form of **land**. God created enough room for Isaac and his family. God blessed him in that land. Isaac became very rich in the land.

*Dwell in the land, and I will be with you and bless you; for to you and your descendants I give all **these lands**, and I will perform the oath I swore to Abraham your father.*

Genesis 26:3

Even Jacob who was a son to Isaac also understood the importance of owning property. When he came to the city of Shechem, which is in the land of Canaan, he bought property. *And he bought the parcel of land, where he had pitched his tent, from the children of Hamor, Shechem's father.*

Genesis 33:19

God also gave him land in Bethel as an inheritance. "*The land which I gave Abraham and Isaac I give you; and to your descendants after you I give this land*"

Genesis 35:12

God also gave Israel property as a promise. He gave them prime land, buildings, houses that they did not build vineyards and orange groves. Even King David also understood this principle that God wants his children to own properties. That is land, buildings, cities and vineyards. *David also defeated Hadadezer the son of Rehob, King of Zobah, as he went to recover his* **territory** *at the river Euphrates.*

2 Samuel 8:3

When King David took over the reigns as king over all the tribes of Israel he started to recover all the land which had been taken away by the Philistines, Moabites, Syrians, Ammonites and Amalekites. He understood that he had to fight to possess more land. He had to extend the boundaries of his kingdom to the River Euphrates. David demonstrated that you have to fight to possess the land that belongs to you.

The king extended the land so as to extend his kingdom. He even fought battles to recover lost land. Land was important to him. You should not allow the devil to take your property. You have to recover what was stolen from you. It is God's pleasure that we regain what the devil has stolen from you. You should never allow him to possess your pleasant mountains. You have to remove all barriers that come your way so as to possess your pleasant mountains. You have to drive out all your adversaries who want to occupy your pleasant mountains.

CHAPTER 3

EMPOWERED TO POSSESS

You are a great people and have great power...

Joshua 17:17

The children of Joseph saw themselves as great people. Indeed God had given them greatness. Jacob had prophesied about them many decades before about their greatness. He spoke greatness into the lives through their ancestor Joseph. The Lord had given them strength to win. They had been empowered to possess their pleasant mountains in the land of Canaan decades before they came to the Promised Land.

The Lord had made them to be mighty warriors who could defeat any army. The Lord wanted them to utterly destroy all the nations which were staying in the Promised Land. He made their arms to be strong and had empowered them to possess the hilly country that was their lot and share.… *And the arms of his hands were made strong by the hands of the Mighty God of Jacob. The blessings of your father have excelled the blessings of my ancestors up to the utmost bound of everlasting hills.*

Genesis 49:24-26

The same prophecy was repeated by Moses the servant of the Lord. By repeating the same prophecy God was showing the children of Joseph that He would fulfil what he had promised. And of Joseph he said: "Blessed *of the Lord is his land, with the best things of ancient mountains, with the precious things of the everlasting hills, with the precious things of the earth and its fullness, and the favour of him who dwelt in the bush…*

Deuteronomy 33:15-16

The children of Joseph were given the ancient mountains and the everlasting hills before they were born. They were destined to possess the hills and mountains in the Promised Land through their father Joseph. Joshua gave them the hills and mountains as their lot and share when they came to the Promised Land. They named the mountains after Joseph's son called Ephraim.

These mountains were covered by the woods and the Canaanites, Perizzites and the giants were staying in the valleys had iron chariots. The children of Joseph were afraid of the giants and the weapons that the Canaanites had. The giants were staying in the mountains and the Canaanites were occupying the valleys. They therefore thought that they could not possess their lot. Little they know that they had been empowered to possess them. The prophecy says their hands had been made strong for war. They were empowered to win any war by the God of their father Jacob. This story shows that you have born into greatness. What limits you to reach your destiny is fear of circumstances around you. You conclude that you are not able to do great things in this world. As a result you can live a life of murmuring and complaints. You then blame other people for your fears and failures.

The mountains seemed not to be able to have enough room for them but they could extend it to the end of the hills by cutting down the woods. God had destined them for the best lot. They were given the best things of the earth and the hills. The hills were rich in mineral wealth. They needed understanding of what the Lord had put on the inside of them. Their lot was well resourced with minerals, milk and honey. They also had arable land in the valleys of Jezreel and around the cities and towns of Beth Shean.

However when the children of Joseph came to the pleasant mountains they found that the occupants had iron chariots. These were powerful weapons of their time. This brought fear among the children of Joseph. They therefore complained to their leader called Joshua. Fear and dread of the Canaanites had fallen on them. They immediately forgot who they were. They were destined to be great warriors who could easily drive out any adversity.

Fear brought in unbelief. They forgot that the mighty God of Jacob would fight for them. The Lord had defeated the Egyptians, Amalek, Og, Bashan and had brought down the walled city of Jericho. The Angel of the Lord had always gone before them to fight for them. All they had to do was to fight the enemies knowing that they were empowered to drive out the Canaanites, Perizzites and the giants with their iron chariots.

The children of Joseph had to confront their fears in order to drive out the enemies. This shows you that what make you fail to achieve greatness are your fears. You can achieve anything that you put your minds as long as you are able to confront our fears. You have been empowered to achieve great things in life. Man was able to send people into space because he discovered that he had been empowered by God to do great things. Man was able to walk on the moon on the 20th of July 1969 because he realised that he had been empowered to do exploits in life. You might not walk on the moon like Neil Armstrong and Edwin Aldrin but you can achieve great things in your career, ministry or family because you have been empowered to possess your pleasant mountains.

Neil Armstrong was the first person to ever set his foot on the moon. He was able to do what no other man had done before. He had been empowered by the Lord to do great things as an austranut. He understood who he was. This revelation enabled him to make history. He was able to experience what no other person had ever experienced before. He was able to possess his pleasant mountains. He walked on the moon!

Another trend setter was a man in the bible who instructed the sun and the moon to stand still and delayed its setting for twenty four hours! His name was Joshua. Joshua was in a battle and he could see that he did not have enough time to defeat his enemies before sunset. He needed the light of day so that his enemies who not escape at night. He therefore did the unthinkable. He told the sun to stand still. Now we know that the sun does not move. Therefore he instructed the earth to stop its rotation for twenty four hours! Both the sun and the moon stopped till he had won the battle. What an amazing achievement for someone who was seen as just a servant to the man of God called Moses...*sun stand still over Gibeon; and moon, in the valley of Aijalon. So the sun stood still, and the moon stopped, till the people had revenge upon their enemies.* Joshua 10:12-13

This scripture shows that you have been empowered to do the unthinkable. You are born to be successful in life. Do not let fear limit you from your God given destiny. You are well able to possess your pleasant mountains. Joshua made this declaration in the presence of the children of Israel. He knew who he was. He had been empowered to possess his pleasant mountains. God made him a mighty man of valour. God has also given you a special gift that you ought to activate. You can change this world if you understand that you have the DNA of a victor. You cannot lose and no one can stop you. Greatness is a guaranteed for any project that you put your mind to.

Characteristics of a winner

- Stand on God's promises.
  God spoke to the children of Joseph a prophecy by their father Jacob. He told them that their hands had been made strong for war. The same prophecy was repeated by Moses, the man of God.

This showed that this prophecy would indeed come to pass. God had to repeat the prophecy as an assurance to the children of Joseph. He knew they would want to doubt what they had been empowered to do. All they needed to do was to stand on God's promises in the form of prophecy. Success is guaranteed for anyone who stands on what God's promises. The Lord will see to it that what He has promised will surely come to pass.

- Study the word of God
  God showed us that if we are to be successful in life we had to read the word of God. We also have to meditate on the word all the time and to be doers of the word. True success in life comes by doing what God said in His word. You need to study the word of God and then speak it out from your spirit. The word of God will always bring prosperity and good success. *This book of the Law shall not depart from your mouth, but you shall meditate in it day and night, that you may observe to do according to all that is written in it. For then shall you make your prosperous, and then you will have good success.*

  Joshua 1:8

- The Lord is on your side.
  A winner knows that the Lord is always on his/her side. He promises us that He will never leave us nor forsake us. He promised the children of Israel that He would be with them at all times. Therefore there was no reason for fear to trickle in. the Lord has given his spirit to living inside His people. Do not fear anything for the Lord is with you and He will fight for you.

  …do not be dismayed, for the Lord your God is with you wherever you go

  Joshua 1:9

- Confront your fears
  It is human nature to complain whenever we are faced with situations that seem impossible. We tend to focus on the reasons

why we cannot overcome certain challenges in life. As we focus on these challenges they become bigger and bigger. We then murmur and complain. We then try to shift the blame to others. The children of Joseph blamed Joshua. They blamed him for giving them a small lot which was occupied by people who had powerful weapons. Their focus was on what they could not do rather on their strength as a nation which had been empowered to reign. They wanted Joshua to do something for them without the revelation that they were able to overcome their challenges. *But the mountain country is yours. Although it is wooded, you shall cut it down, and its farthest extent shall be yours; for you shall drive out the Canaanites, though they have iron chariots and are strong.*

Joshua 17:8

Joshua reminded them of their strengths. He told them what they had been empowered to do and to have. He told them that the mountain belonged to them. They had to extend the mountains by clearing the forests and ultimately defeating the giants. He told them to confront their fears so that they would be able to possess their pleasant mountains.

The children of Joseph had been empowered to do the impossible. They were born to be successful. Do not live your life believing that they you are just ordinary. Never murmur, complain or live in fear of the challenges that come your way. You were never meant for a life of mediocrity. The good Lord has put greatness on the inside. You are born already empowered to be great.

Esther

Now the king was attracted to Esther more than to any of the other women, and she won his favour and approval more than any of the other virgins. So he set a royal crown on her head and made her queen…

Esther 2:7

Esther was born at a time when the Jews were living in exile. They had been defeated and carried away into captivity in Babylon. Esther had lost both parents. She faced insurmountable challenges as a teenage orphan living in a foreign land. It looked like she was going to have an ordinary life. Her future looked bleak. Maybe she would be a maid serving the Babylonians all of her life.

When Esther was born her parents understood that she had a great destiny. They therefore named her Hadassah. Hadassah means perfume. The name came from the word Hadas which is a myrtle tree. This tree has a pleasant fragrance. No one would ignore the fragrance produced by the Myrtle tree. Hadassah was empowered to receive the favour of all people. The name Hadassah also means light, bride, queen or a star. So the parents had a revelation that she had been empowered to become a queen. She was born with a lovely figure and she was very beautiful. These were key attributes for a queen.

Esther was born in captivity which meant that there was no way she could become queen in a foreign land. But God works in mysterious ways. His ways are not our ways. Esther changed her name Hadassah so as to conceal her true identity that she was a foreigner. Her name was changed to Esther. The name Esther means hidden. Her nationality was hidden as it would block her from achieving her destiny. She therefore grew up like any other ordinary girl who had beautiful looks and a lovely physical appearance. Esther was programmed by God from the beginning to be a wife of a king but because Esther means hidden, her beauty was hidden all these years. When the time came for her promotion the queen at that time misbehaved. Her name was Queen Vashti. She made one big mistake which led to her removal as a queen. The leaders then decided to hold a beauty contest as a process of selecting a replacement. Many girls entered the contest. But only one had been empowered to become a queen. That was Hadassah; the light that had remained hidden as Esther. She was the only girl who had been empowered by God to become the next queen.

At the end of the beauty contest, Esther (Hadassah) won the competition. Her beauty and destiny could not be hidden to the world. This shows us that there is no competition when you pursue what God has purposed for your life. She was chosen as the next queen. This shows us that you ought not to focus on the challenges that come your way but rather to identify your God given destiny.

Then you should focus on what you have been empowered to do. Recognise what you have and focus on your strengths. You must see yourself as a winner. Queen Vashti had to be removed from her position because the one who had been empowered to be queen had now reached the age of marriage. Her destiny was stronger than her challenges. These challenges could not hide her for life. The challenges that you face cannot block you from reaching your God given destiny.

You have been born to possess your pleasant mountains. Do not focus on voices that say you cannot do it. All the woods and iron chariots cannot stop you to walk into your destiny. You are an overcomer. You are the apple of God's eye. Go ahead and possess your pleasant mountains. You can achieve anything that you want. Ask God to show you your pleasant mountains.

CHAPTER 4

HIDDEN TREASURE

*The mountain country shall be yours. Although
it is wooded, you shall cut it down…*

Joshua 17:8

After many years the descendants of Abraham came to the land of Canaan.
They could not wait to inherit the land that the Lord had promised many
years ago to their forefather Abraham. It was now time to possess the
pleasant mountains. Many of the children of Israel thought that it was
going to be easy to inherit the Promised Land. It was going to be a walk
in the park for them. Finally they would enjoy milk and honey just as God
had promised to their fathers.

Their leader at that time was called Joshua. He allotted land to them according to their families. Reuben, Gad and half-tribe of Manasseh got land on the east of the Jordan River. This was land outside of the Promised Land. God's Promised Land was on the western side of the Jordan River. The tribes that were allotted land on the western side of the Jordan were Judah, Ephraim and west Manasseh, Benjamin, Simeon, Zebulun, Issachar, Asher, Naphtali and Dan.

The first tribe to inherit land on the western side was Judah. Judah was followed by the children of Joseph, Ephraim and the other half tribe of Manasseh. This half tribe of Manasseh is also called west Manasseh. The children of joseph or tribes of Joseph comprised of the children of Ephraim and Manasseh. This was one of the largest tribes according to population. God had blessed them and the tribes had grown big by the time that they got to the Pleasant Mountains in the land of Canaan.

The land was to be divided in proportion to the size of the family. The larger tribes would get larger portions of land to inherit. The children of Joseph had been promised more one portion as their inheritance by their forefather Jacob. *Moreover I have given to you one portion above your brothers, which I took from the hand of the Amorite with my sword and my bow.*

Genesis 48:22

The children of joseph complained to Joshua because they wanted a bigger portion as had been promised to bigger tribes. The children of Joseph were a great people who obviously deserved a bigger portion. They claimed that the portion they had been given was too small for them. *And the children of Joseph spoke to Joshua, saying, "Why have you given me only one lot and one share to inherit, seeing I am a great people, forasmuch as the Lord hath blessed me hitherto?"*

Joshua 17:14

The tribes of Joseph were given good land which was made up of hills, mountains and valleys. However when they were given their portion they could only inhabit the hills. The mountains were wooded and the Canaanites were living in the valleys. Therefore a large part of the portion was inhabitable. This was not the milk and honey they had expected. Their pleasant mountains were covered by forests and inhabited by Canaanites who had iron chariots. This brought frustration and disappointment.

But actually the children of Joseph were not given the hills only. They could also have the valleys and plains surrounding the hills. It was their choice to have plains or not to have. They were limited by their fear of the iron chariots and laziness. They could also enjoy the fresh waters of the hillside streams. The hills could also be good defence sites during times of war. The plains had fertile soils for both pastoral and arable farming. This could produce enough food for the nation of Israel. This was a perfect portion. The land was perfect for raising sheep, goats and cattle. They could have meat, milk, cheese and yoghurt.

The tribes of Joseph saw their portion as small and useless because it was a wooded country. The land was full of trees. Therefore they could not occupy their pleasant mountains because they were hidden by forests. Joshua expected them to look at the land with spiritual eyes. Their portion was not as small as they claimed. This land could be enlarged by cutting the trees. The tribes of joseph could therefore have the hillsides and the adjacent valleys and plains. They could therefore practice both arable and pastoral farming.

God has given you gifts that you need to develop. The time you stop complaining is the time you shall see how beautiful you are. It is the time when you realise how blessed you are. The children of Joseph did not see the beauty of the portion of land allotted to them. The children of Joseph did not have the whole view of the land. Their view was obscured by the woods. Their treasure was hidden in the mountain forests. This made the children of Joseph to complain.

Joshua had a bigger and better view. Remember he was one of the twelve spies sent to spy out the land by Moses when they were still in Kadesh

Barnea (Numbers 13:16). He knew that this was a good portion. He had walked through the hills, valleys and mountains. He had seen the fruit of the land. They brought back the grapes, pomegranates and the figs to their leader Moses. Their view was not blocked by the woods.

The children of Joseph needed to understand that their portion was allotted by lot. This was not Joshua's personal decision. This was land given to them through a divine method. It was God's choice for them to get the mountain portion. God's choice is always the best. God gives the best. We get the best if we accept that God does not give substandard things. God promised a good and a large land centuries before the children of Joseph came to the land of Canaan.

Good things come from the Lord. God has given you gifts. They might be covered in the woods. You need to look at what God has given you from his perspective. Some gifts need refining to bring out the best. You have been given the ability to refine your gifts. You refine your gifts through education and experience. Education and experience prepares you to be able to handle bigger assignments.

And Jesus passed by, he saw a man which was blind from his birth. And his disciples asked Him, saying, Master, who did sin, this man, or his parents, that he was born blind? Jesus answered, neither hath this man sinned, nor his parents: but that the works of God should be made manifest in him.

John 9:1-3

The parents of the blind man wanted a baby. Maybe they had prayed and fasted for their child. However when the child was born he was born blind. This was not the pleasant mountain that they had asked God in prayer. This is not what the parents had expected. This was not what they had believed for. Surely God had let them down. They did not know that their son had been born with gifts hidden in the disability.

Jesus explained that people see blindness and think that the person is useless. But it was God himself who had allowed such a condition so that His greatness could be seen. Jesus explained that whatever situation you face is an opportunity for God's works to be made manifest. God can change any situation, in any situation that seems to be unfair call upon God to intervene. Take time to polish your own diamond to get the best form of jewellery. The children of Joseph saw the wooded hills and complained. God saw milk, honey, iron, olives, figs and a good and a large land hidden in the woods.

The children of Joseph saw limitations but Joshua saw opportunities. The children of Joseph saw a small piece of land surrounded by forests. Joshua saw the chance to extend the wooded hills by cutting the trees. Sometimes God's gifts are wrapped in challenges. See beyond what the physical eye can see to enjoy your gift. You cannot see your milk and honey because they are hidden by the giants, iron chariots and the woods.

Rhulani Baloyi

Rhulani Baloyi was born in a small village called Elim, near Louis Trichardt in Limpopo province of South Africa. She was born blind. Some people thought that nothing good would come out of this blind girl. But when people see blindness God sees a masterpiece. Hidden inside this blind girl was a great jewel. Rhulani went on to become a news journalist and talk show host with the South African Broadcasting Corporation (SABC). She presented a highly celebrated youth talk show programme called SHIFT on SABC 1and Intune on SAFM. Obviously when she was born blind it was milk and honey in the woods. But God had put treasure inside her for greatness. She was indeed hidden treasure. Rhulani was able to use her gift to become great even though she had been born blind. She did not allow disability to limit her from reaching her God given destiny. She was able to possess her pleasant mountains in the midst of challenges.

This story shows us that everyone has hidden treasure in them from the Lord almighty. You need to identify what you have been given even though people might not see what you carry. Noone is born as an accident to God. He knew you were coming and he gave you a gift which I call your pleasant mountains. Do not complain and fel sorry for yourself if you were born in disability. Instead discover what you carry so that you can share with the world. Disability does not mean inability. Your spirit is just like anyone else. Your spirit is not disabled. Your mind is not disabled. Go out and share your talent with the world. God is about to shock this worls just as He did with Rhulani.

CHAPTER 5

WHAT DO YOU SEE?

Why have you given us only one lot and one share to inherit…?

Joshua 17:14

The sons of Joseph saw one lot and one share only. Their inheritance was covered by the woods. They therefore complained to the man of God Joshua. They saw that that the portion allotted to them was too small for them since they were a great nation. This was contrary to what God had promised. He had promised a large and a good land. The tribe of Joseph was a large tribe. They therefore deserved a bigger lot and share. Joshua seemed to have overlooked this reality.

There are times in life when you live in mediocrity because you fail to see what the Lord has blessed you with. You see and exaggerate the obstacles that you face in trying to fulfil your dreams. You feel that you deserve to have a better life. The key is to take the positives from any situation or challenge and focus on it. God does not give substandard things to His beloved children. Life is like an echo from a mountain. You get positive things if you say positive words and think positively.

The children of Joseph also saw that their lot was inhabited by Canaanites who had iron chariots. Iron chariots were dangerous weapons of the day. The Canaanites were therefore very strong and powerful. These Canaanites were staying in the valley and the towns. The children of Joseph could see danger in the towns of Beth Shean and the valley of Jezreel. The sons of Joseph saw injustice and impending defeat. This was not the pleasant mountains that they had been promised.

The children of Joseph saw themselves as being disadvantaged. Joshua had allotted them land in a place where the inhabitants had iron chariots. Iron chariots were a devastating weapon. The children saw that it was not going to be easy to possess their inheritance. They were afraid of the iron chariots. They saw themselves as being unable to possess their lot.

The children of Joseph failed to acknowledge that God was able to fight for them. They did not trust in their God. They did not believe that God was able to fight for them. The Lord had fought and brought a great victory for Israel at the Red sea against Pharaoh's army that had 600 chariots. The same God would bring victory for the children of Joseph. He had drowned Pharaoh's chariots in the Red sea. He had destroyed all the well trained Egyptian soldiers with their chariots in one battle. *"Then the waters returned and covered the chariots, the horsemen, and all the army of Pharaoh that came into the sea after them. Not so much as one of them remained".*

Exodus 14:28

Pharaoh's chariots and his army He has cast into the sea; His chosen captains are also drowned in the Red Sea.

Exodus 15:4

It is also important to note that the children of Joshua tried to use public opinion. They said why you have given "us" a small piece of land. What is important in life is what you see as an individual. You have personal dreams that you would like to see coming true. Sometimes you let the crowd define what you see in your future. The crowd define your circumstances, situations and aspirations and conclude that you are not good enough to possess your pleasant mountains.

You need to stick to what you see in your future as an individual. You were created for greatness. I see success and victory in your future. I see a company with your name. I see a book with your name. I see your children graduating from college. I see a big church where many people are giving their lives to Jesus. I see a great future ahead of you. I see you sticking to what the Lord has declared in His word and you will do exploits for Him.

The children of Joseph saw a limitation. However the man of God saw differently. He saw a bigger lot still covered by woods. He told them to clear the woods to create a bigger portion. Joshua said that their land was not small. The sons of Joshua would clear the forest and occupy the mountain country up to the farthest extent of the portion allotted to them. He told them to drive out the Canaanites even though they had iron chariots. In other words Joshua told them to possess their pleasant mountains.

This shows us that you ought to look at issues with the eyes of faith. God works with what you see. If we expand your view you will certainly be able to possess your pleasant mountains. You will get more from your heavenly father. He has prepared pleasant mountains for you to possess as His children. The bible says

"Eye has not seen, nor ear heard,

Nor have entered into the heart of man

The things which God has prepared for those who love Him

1 Corinthians 2:9

Jeremiah

God works upon what you see. He has prepared wonderful things for your enjoyment. God does not want you to be limited in your thinking. He wants you to have a bigger view. God asked the same question before He could use prophet Jeremiah. *Moreover the word of the Lord came to me, saying, Jeremiah, what do you see? And I said, "I see a branch of an almond tree".*

Jeremiah 1:11

This seems to suggest that God works as far as you can see. That is why Joshua told the sons of Joseph that they could extend their portion by clearing the woods and driving out the Canaanites. God would give them victory over their enemies if they saw victory. God will also give you victory according to what you see in the spirit.

Abraham

God had the same message to Abraham. *"Lift your eyes now and look from the place where you are-northward, southward, eastward, and westward; for all the land which you see I give to you and your descendants forever.*

Genesis 13:14-15

God told Abraham that He would give him a land as big as he was able to see. The size of his inheritance would be determined by what he saw by lifting up his eyes. This principle still works today. The bigger land you see in the spirit is proportional to what God would give you in the physical. If you see a small portion then God also gives a small portion. It is there imperative that you see situations and circumstances that you face in life through the eyes of the spirit. What you see with your physical eyes is temporal. It is subject to change. There is more to what you see with your optical eyes.

Lot chose the plains of Jordan which were in the east. He saw that it was well watered. He focused his eyes on the green pastures for his flocks and herds. He saw the green pastures in the physical. He moved eastwards towards the city of Sodom where the people were evil. Later this city was destroyed for their evil deeds by the Lord. He did not see the problems which were coming because he used the physical eyes. What he saw was temporal. He did not sense any danger. The use of his optical eyes would eventually lead to his demise.

Abraham was left in the much drier land when Lot chose the well-watered eastern plains. In the physical nothing good would come out of that land. But out of this seemingly arid and useless land would come out great things. All Abraham had to do was to lift his eyes and see with the eyes of the spirit. God later gave it to Abraham and his descendants as an inheritance. What Lot saw as useless and unable to sustain his flocks and herds was in fact the land that God gave to Abraham and his descendants. God reminded Abraham that he in fact had the better portion of land. All he needed to do what to see it with the eyes of the spirit. Do not face on the challenges that you are facing. Lift your own eyes and the see your pleasant mountains that God has prepared for you.

Elisha

"Nevertheless, if you see me when I am taken from you, it shall be so far for you; but if not, it shall not be so"

2 Kings 2:10

Elisha asked for a double portion of Elijah's spirit. Elijah told Elisha that it was only possible if he would see him being taken away. Elijah told Elisha that he could only get what he wanted if he saw him being taken away. This shows that what you see is instrumental to what we can achieve in life. What do you see in your future?

What do you see in your situations, circumstances? You need to pray to

God to open our eyes so that you can see the way He sees. I pray, Lord open my eyes to see. The children of Joseph had to see themselves winning against a much stronger opponent. God would give them victory only if they saw themselves driving out the Canaanites. This shows that your success in life is proportional to what you see with your spiritual eyes. You can do great things if only you see yourself as a great person. This will increase your confidence levels as you see your victory.

CHAPTER 6

ENLARGE THE BOUNDARY OF YOUR PLEASANT MOUNTAINS

Joshua answered them, "if thou be a great people, then get thee up to the wood country, and cut down for thyself there in the land of the Perizzites and of the giants, if mount Ephraim be too narrow for thee".

Joshua 17:15

The sons of Joseph complained about the portion of land that had been allotted to them. This portion was too small for their large and great tribe. What they saw was a portion that was not enough for them. The land was hilly, wooded and in it dwelt the Canaanites, Perizzites and the giants who had iron chariots. The sons of Joseph were afraid of the iron chariots. The Canaanites were huge in stature. They thought that they could not defeat the giants.

The tribes of Joseph did not know that they had to fight to inherit their promise. Their treasure was covered by the woods. They had to cut the woods to enlarge their portion. Joshua told the tribe of Joseph that they had to do something about their situation. They were not just to mourn, complain and murmur. They were not to complain that the hill was too small and the people had iron chariots. Joshua said that the children of Joseph had to show their greatness. Great people do not complain but they fight the adversary. Joshua says enlarge your territory if it is too small for you. Go and cut the woods and drive out the people. You are well able to possess your pleasant mountains.

Joshua reminded the sons of Joseph that what was important was not the great stature of their enemies but the greatness that God had put inside them. The man of God reminded them that they were a great people who had the ability to defeat their enemies. They were born great and clearly deserved a bigger share of land. He reminded them not to be limited by what they saw on the outside. He told them that they could extend the little that they saw. He told them to drive out the enemy so as to get a bigger portion.

The answer was to clear the wooded hills to create more room for themselves. He reminded them that they had the power to possess and own the farthest extent of their country. He told them that there was more to what they were seeing. Their treasure was hidden in the woods. They had to fight their fears to get their promise. They had to fight the Canaanites with their chariots of iron in order to possess their pleasant mountains. The sons of Joseph had to drive out all their fears, challenges and limitations. This would be a sign of true greatness.

The tribes of Joseph did not know that greatness is not in consumption but in production. A great nation is one that produces goods for her citizens and for export to other countries. All great countries in this world are net exporters. A great nation adds value to the resources that God has blessed them with. The citizens of a great nation add value to what God has provided. They are able to possess their pleasant mountains.

If you want to possess your pleasant mountains you have a winning mentality. This mentality will enable you to extend the boundaries of your portion so that you will have enough room to settle. It is easy to conquer if you have a winning mentality. Failure is not an option for champions. Greatness is in the mind of champions. To be successful you need to have a strong mentality. Joshua told the children of Joseph to be strong because God had given them great power. We need to wake up and work to make it in life. Joshua told the tribes of Ephraim and Manasseh that they could have the hills as their portion. All they needed to do was to cut down the trees, as woodcutters to enlarge their land. They were not supposed to sit and mourn. Idleness is a major contributor to poverty among many people. They sit, complain, mourn and murmur. However this does not change their situation.

There are times when you want God to intervene in your situations and yet he has given you all that we need. Sometimes you fail to see beyond your wooded mountains and valleys as it were. You want God to do more because you deserve more. God has already given you gifts. At times you fail to see the treasure that God has given you because of the woods covering them. Therefore you have to cut down the trees and enlarge your territory. That is why some people say that you cannot enjoy honey if you are afraid of bees.

Sometimes you feel intimidated by the challenges that you face not realising that God has made you bigger than your challenges. To enjoy life you have to work our way through the adversity. Joshua told the children of Joseph that they had to drive the Canaanites from their portion so as to possess their pleasant mountains. He told them that they were able to do it. Joshua told them that they had the numbers and had they already confessed greatness. Therefore they were well able to create more room that they needed

Even when Jacob was blessing Joseph he told him that he could occupy the pleasant mountains up to the boundaries of the everlasting hills (Genesis

49:24). Jacob saw these hills in his spirit when he was blessing his son Joseph. He saw the mountains of Ephraim years before his grandchildren inherited the mountains. He even saw the minerals underneath these mountains. The mountains had copper and iron which would benefit the children of Joseph. *And the almighty who will bless you…blessings of the deep that lies beneath*

Genesis 49:25

The tribes of Joseph had been given the ability to drive out the Canaanites regardless of their iron chariots. *And the arms of his hands were made strong by the hands of the Mighty God of Jacob.*

Genesis 49:24

God had prepared Israel for battle many generations before they came into Canaan. They had been enabled to drive out the Perizzites and the Canaanites with their iron chariots. This shows that you are born to win, succeed and to influence in Jesus Name. Amen.

God had made them victors. It was their mentality that was wrong. God made them to great but they were fearful. God had invested in Israel for 40 years in the wilderness. He had shown them His mighty hand. He had supernaturally fed them with the bread from heaven. He had refreshed them with water from a rock. He gave them meat in the desert. But still the children of Israel had the wrong attitude.

A person born with greatness inside can become a failure due to wrong attitude. Greatness was put inside the children of Joseph. They even declared themselves great. They understood that they were born great. However what they failed to understand was the fact that the same God who put greatness inside them had already given them the ability to defeat their adversary with their iron chariots.

Success was not going to be determined by the iron chariots that the Canaanites had but God's promise. When God makes a promise he brings it to pass. Joshua says to the children of Joseph you have to fight to enjoy your pleasant mountains. Joshua says to the children of Joseph you are well able to do it. You have been made to succeed. You were designed to excel. *But you are a chosen generation, a royal priesthood, a holy nation, His own special people, that you may proclaim the praises of Him who called you out of darkness into His marvellous light.*

1 Peter 2:9

All successful people in this world have a positive self-portrait. When they look in the mirror they see a winner, a champion. David was one of the greatest kings of Israel. He had a positive self-portrait. He saw victory before he fought Goliath. He spoke to the giant saying, *"This day will the Lord deliver thee into mine hand; I will smite thee, and take thine head from thee; and I will give the carcasses of the host of the Philistines this day unto the fowls of the air, and to the wild beasts of the earth…*

1 Samuel 17:46

All the soldiers were afraid of the giant. No-one was prepared to fight the giant. All the soldiers were afraid of the enemy. David did not have a military uniform or weapons to fight with. He was not a trained soldier in Saul's army. He was trained by God when he was looking after his father's flock of sheep. He knew that all he needed was the name of the Lord. He knew that he had been born to win. He had developed a positive self-portrait in the wilderness as a shepherd boy. With a positive self-portrait you are unstoppable in this world.

To succeed in life you need to be passionate about what you do. Passion is a driving force behind a person with a gift. David had the passion to do exploit for God. Passion enabled him to defeat the giant called Goliath for Israel. He was excited at the prospect of defeating the giant. He asked for the benefits of defeating Goliath. David was passionate because he knew that God never fails. He had faith that God would do it again, as he had done with the lion and the bear. His faith was based on what God had already done.

The children of Joseph had seen the hand of the Lord in the wilderness. As young children they had seen the outstretched hand of the Lord. God had fed them on heavenly bread. God had provided water from a rock. God had given them meat in the wilderness. God had sweetened the bitter Marah waters. God had defeated the seven kings. The same God would do it again.

Against all odds

There are situations that you face in life that seem insurmountable. All it takes is a personal attitude that takes the positives out of every adverse situation and move forward. You can change any adverse condition that you face in life and be able to possess your pleasant mountains. Any tough situation that you face in life is not permanent. You need to continue with a positive mind set so that you can change the situations or circumstances into a life of victory. There are many people who have gone through tough situations that you can use to inspire others. They were able to possess their pleasant mountains regardless of their circumstances.

Natalie du Toit

One person who managed to make it in life against all odds is Natalie du Toit. She was able to extend her boundaries despite the life threatening car accident. Natalie was hit by car while riding her scooter after swimming practice in 2001. After the accident her leg was amputated at the knee. She did not sit and mourn about the accident. But she strengthened herself and continued swimming. She says, *"Even when bad things happen you have to try to use those bad things in a positive manner and really just take the positive out of it"*

She went on to become one of the best paralympians in the world. Three years after the accident she won five gold medals at the 2004 Athens Paralympics. Natalie was also chosen to carry the South African flag at the Opening Ceremony of the 2008 Beijing Olympic Games. She became the first athlete to carry a flag at both Olympics and Paralympics in a single year. This shows that we can succeed regardless of any circumstances that we face. But only if we understand that we were created to succeed. We can extend our boundaries regardless of the circumstances surrounding us.

Do not allow any temporary setbacks to block you from reaching your destiny. Do not allow a car accident, job loss, divorce, a sickness or death of a spouse to stop you from living a life of victory and success. It is just a temporary setback. Shake it off and move forward like what Natalie did. There is an Olympic medal with your name after the accident. There is a flag to carry after what people would call a major seatback. There is a company with your name on it after being retrenched from work. There is a PhD gown waiting for you after failing your first semester as an undergraduate.

Professor Shirley Zinn

Shirley Zinn was born and grew up in the Cape flats in South Africa. This was a place known for gangsters, alcoholism and teenage pregnancy. She was born in a harsh environment in which not many people would do well at school. It was a tough environment for a girl child to grow up in. Many girls would fall into drugs or fall pregnant at a young age. Most boys joined gangs and lived rough lifestyles. Most young people would were not able to far with their academic studies. But against all odds, Shirley was able to succeed in academics. She went on to obtain a PhD from the prestigious Harvard University in the United States of America.

She went on to have an incredible academic career and became a business executive. She also owns her own companies. She utilised all the opportunities that came through her life out of this seemingly hopeless environment. She had a vision of her life. She could see into her future in which she could positively influence her tough neighbourhood. This would be a future where she could also inspire others to succeed in life out of adverse environments. She managed to possess her "pleasant mountains".

She was able to use all the opportunities that came her way regardless of her adverse situations. *But it was in taking the first step, and removing the "I can't "message from my mind, that the opportunity presented itself. I believe that many opportunities are missed if one is not tuned in or receptive to the possibilities that may emerge.*

Do not sit and blame your background. You are well able to succeed regardless of how hard your environment is. Shirley has shown that you should not allow your background to determine your future. You can all achieve your dreams if you have the right attitude. You are stronger than your environment. You have to decide to be different from others. God has put greatness in you regardless of the place where you were born or where you grew up in. Identify all the possibilities that come your way and take advantage. There is a PhD gown waiting for you at Harvard or any other university. You are well able to do it regardless of your age, sex, race, background or nationality.

Write your vision

Writing down your vision helps you to be strong during hard times. God prepares you for the vision that he gives you. Between your vision and the time it is fulfilled there will be tough times. When you go through tough times refer back to the vision or dream that you wrote down. Dreams take different times to come to pass. The training for a bigger vision is longer than a smaller vision.

The Joshua said to the children of Israel: how long will you neglect to go and possess the land which the Lord God of your fathers has given you? Pick out from among you three men for each tribe, and I will send them; they shall rise and go through the land, survey it according to their inheritance, and come back to me."

Joshua 18:3-4

Joshua called each tribe to choose three men to form part of the investigating team. This team had to pass through the land and describe it. The team members were supposed to survey and then draw a map of the land. God had already given them the land. However in order for them to succeed in inheriting the land they needed to walk through the land. They had to describe the land in their own words. There is power in seeing. There is power in words. *Death and life are in the power of the tongue*

Proverbs 18:21

What you confess is what you get.

Joshua had been part of an earlier mission sent out to spy the land by Moses, the man of God. They had travelled throughout the land. He had seen the land and he knew how beautiful and big the land was. When you describe the land you have to write advantages of the land. This helps one to appreciate the beauty of the land. It is important to write the vision that God gives you. Write down all the idea, the dreams that you have in life. One day it shall come to pass.

God said the same thing to Abram when he said, *"Arise, walk through the land in the length of it and in the breadth of it; for I will give it unto thee.*

Genesis 13:17

It was going to be difficult for Abram to walk through this land physically but it would be possible to do it in spirit. See yourself living your dreams. Write down where you see yourself in ten years, in twenty years or in fifty years. The vision that God has for your life is big. God gave Joseph dreams to show that one day he would be a leader.

"And there remained among the children of Israel seven tribes which had not yet received their inheritance".

Joshua 18:2

There are many people today who believe that they are not good enough to be successful in life. As a result they live mediocre lives. Many people died with their given gifts, talents and visions because they saw the Canaanites with the iron chariots. Peoples, who were supposed to have written books, plays, started businesses, brought new inventions into this world died without fulfilling their dreams. They saw the woods, iron chariots, hills and mountains. They saw huge mountains to climb, deep rivers to cross. They were limited by negative circumstances.

Do not be limited by the system

There are many people who live their lives as victims not victors. They are enslaved by the traditions, rules and systems. They live in captivity all their lives limited by the system. They have accepted the status quo as the norm. God has put greatness in you. You can change any situation in your lives. You can move any mountain that was put before us by tradition, rules and systems. You can say to the mountain be moved into the sea. You can change the system and successfully possess your pleasant mountains.

Go Go Girls

Why should the name of our father be removed from among his family because he had no son? Give us a possession among our father's brothers".

Numbers 27:4

The five daughters of Zelophehad came to Moses with a request. Their names were Mahlah, Noah, Hoglah, Milcah and Tirzah. These five girls wanted to inherit their father's land. Their father called Zelophehad had died without sons who could inherit his share of land in the promised land of Canaan according to the culture of the day. These girls made a decision that they could not be limited by the system. They could not be limited by traditional inheritance laws.

According to the current inheritance laws girls were not allowed to inherit land. They were not even allowed to appear before males. Women were supposed to be silent and accept decisions made by men. They were not even counted when Moses held a census. Only sons were counted in the census. Therefore the names of these five girls were not in the system. Only the names of boys who were twenty years or older were in the system.

However these five girls decided to claim their father's inheritance. They made a decision to enlarge their boundaries. They approached Moses and the leaders with their petition. Moses approached God for divine instruction. God approved the girl's request and instructed Moses to give them an inheritance. This changed Israel's inheritance laws. This law was even extended to others to others as well. They opened the doors for others.

And the Lord spoke to Moses, saying: "the daughters of Zelophehad speak what is right; you shall surely give them a possession of inheritance among their father's brothers, and cause the inheritance of their father to pass to them".

Numbers 27:6-7

The five daughters came together and worked as a team. They showed determination and boldness. As females it was intimidating to approach males and a make a demand. They refused to be limited by the system. They were aware of the promise God had made to Abram their forefather. They had studied the law. They knew that it was only boys who could inherit the land. However they refused to be limited by the system.

Other women also benefited as the inheritance laws were changed. From that time women could also inherit land. This became a statute for generations of the children of Israel. *God said to Moses: And you shall speak to the children of Israel, saying: "If a man dies and has no son, then you shall cause his inheritance to pass to his daughter".*

CHAPTER 7

BEYOND THE IRON CHARIOTS

...For you shall drive out the Canaanites, though they have iron chariots and are strong.

Joshua 17:18

The children of Joseph complained about the land that was allotted to them. They were afraid of the iron chariots that the Canaanites had. However Joshua told them to drive out the Canaanites out of the place. They had to fight so that they could receive more land in the valley of

Jezreel. This was a fertile area that could be used for arable farming. The key was to fight for their portion of land

It is important to understand that in life battles that come your way are not meant to destroy you. God has divine rewards in every battle for those who decide to fight and win. A battle is a seed for territory. You have to fight obstacles that come your way to acquire more territory. The children of Joseph were afraid of the iron chariots owned by the Canaanites. What they did not realise was the fact that this challenge was there to create more land for them. Winning a battle is a seed for promotion. The focus should have been on opportunities that this challenge would create and not on the iron chariots.

Benefits of the battle

The children of Joseph would get more land in the valley of Jezreel. They would possess the towns of Beth Shean. They could extend their territory in the mountains. Winning the battle would enable them to extend their land to the farthest extent of their portion. All the hills of Ephraim would be theirs. This would create enough room for the children of Joseph. They would finally enlarge their portion so as to get a large land.

The milk and honey for the sons of Joseph was hidden beyond the iron chariots. Your treasure is hidden beyond what we see in life. You can live your dream in life if you go beyond your circumstances. Success is not determined by your education, background, race or gender but what you have on the inside. Treasure is guaranteed when you drive out your fears and clear your woods.

David

God blessed David as a great warrior and king. His father failed to identify the jewel that God had put in him. He did not even invite him to be present when the prophet Samuel came to anoint one of his sons as a king. He was the official shepherd for the family. Jesse saw David as a shepherd boy not a future king. Samuel saw the future king of Israel. Obviously he was a hidden treasure in the woods.

After being anointed King, David went back to shepherd the family's sheep. There was no-one to launch him to greatness. David seized the opportunity to fight Goliath to launch his career as a warrior and leader. He understood that battles can propel a person to greatness. He wanted God to extend his boundaries. He wanted God to extend his influence in the kingdom. He knew that God would give him victory over the giant. This was his chance to shine.

David understood this principle very well. One day he was sent to the battle front by his father. He was sent to check on his brothers who were at the battle front. His three brothers Eliab, Abinadab and Shammah were in the army. David had to bring back word about his brothers to his father. He had to report how they were doing. After the report he would resume his responsibilities as a shepherd.

When David got to the battle front, he found that all the soldiers were afraid of the giant called Goliath. David was not afraid of the giant. He was afraid of the challenge because he knew that it was his opportunity for promotion. David understood that he would benefit from this challenge. He asked the other soldiers how he would benefit if he won the battle.

The David spoke to the men who stood by him, saying, "What shall be done for the man who kills this Philistine and takes away the approach from Israel? For who is this uncircumcised Philistine, that he should defy the armies of the living God?

1 Samuel 17:26

Benefits of winning the battle

David saw the giant just like everyone who was there. All the soldiers were afraid of this giant. He knew that beyond this giant would be something great. He understood that God had put something great inside him. He knew that God would give him the victory. He asked for the benefits of winning this battle. He knew that not all battles had rewards. He ignored the first battle with his older brother because there were no benefits for winning that battle.

David was told of the three promises that the king had made. This battle had three very important rewards. This was a battle worth fighting for. These benefits were great wealth, marrying the king's daughter and exemption from the payment of taxes for his family.

…and it shall be that the man who kills him the king will enrich with great riches, will give him his daughter, and give his father's house exemption from taxes in Israel.

1 Samuel 17:25

Marrying the King's daughter

After the battle King Saul gave Michal his daughter to become David's wife. By marrying the king's daughter David could therefore occupy an important position in the kingdom as the king's son in law. Just one battle elevated David to prominence. The win over Goliath helped him extend his influence. This win helped him to possess his pleasant mountains.

David was presented before the king

When David won the battle he was brought before the king. From that day he became known by the king. Winning the battle gave him access to the presidency. David was able to come in the presence of the king without an appointment. Winning a battle helps one to break protocol and be known by great people such as kings and presidents. *And Saul said to him (David), "Whose son are you, young man? SO David answered, "I am the son of your servant Jesse the Bethlehemite".*

1 Samuel 17:58

David became an instant celebrity. Winning a battle changed him who was not known into a national champion. The win brought joy to the kingdom. The women composed a song in his honour. The song became the song of the moment in the kingdom. The song became an instant hit. The victory over Goliath enabled David to possess his pleasant mountains.

Many women came to meet their new champion at the international airport. They came in song and dance. Some even had placards with David's photo and name written on them. All the newspapers had David as their lead story. This happened as David was returning from the slaughter of the Philistine. The women came with tambourines, with joy and with musical instruments. So the women sang as they danced, and said:

"Saul has slain his thousands and David his ten thousands"

1 Samuel 17:6-7

David was promoted to the rank of captain

David was promoted after winning the Goliath battle. The king decided to reward him for his bravery. He was promoted to the rank of captain. He was now in charge of a thousand men. This was made possible by the great victory over Goliath the Philistine. Winning the battle brought promotion. David became a leader. He moved from being an ordinary shepherd boy to Captain David.

Therefore Saul removed him from his presence and made him captain over a thousand; and he went out and came in before the people.

1 Samuel 18:13

It is important to realise that a battle is an opportunity for promotion. It is God who fights our battles. It is Him who gives victory. What we need is to acknowledge him. *David said to Goliath, "This day the Lord will deliver you into my hand, and I will strike you and take your head from you. And this day I will give the carcasses of the camp of the Philistines to the wild beasts of the earth, that all the earth may know that there is a God in Israel. Then all this assembly shall know that the Lord does not save with sword and spear; for the battle is the Lord's, and He will give you into our hands".*

1 Samuel 17:46-47

David went to the battle front as a visitor. He came back a champion. He came back as the king's son-in-law. He came back to a family now exempt from paying taxes. Only one battle changed his life and his family forever. He came back as a captain over a thousand men. This is what the children of Joseph failed to understand that the woods, giants and iron chariots were opportunities for promotion. God himself would fight for them and promote them with a good and a large land. Challenges that you face are opportunities for your promotion in life.

The children of Joseph were afraid of the iron chariots of the Canaanites. But Joseph reminded them that they had power to drive out their enemies from the land. God was going to fight for them. There was no need to be afraid. There was no need to complain and do nothing. God would fight the battle for them:

The Lord is a man of war;

The Lord is His name.

Exodus 15:3

The same God is still fighting battles for his children. Acknowledge him and he will fight for you. He will give you victory. He is strong and mighty in battle. He fights for those who acknowledge him. There is no need to cry, complain or to be fearful. He will redeem you from destruction. Your safety is in him. He is your shield. God can extend your boundaries. He is your deliverer. *The righteous cry out, and the Lord hears and delivers them of all their troubles* Psalm 34:17

Jabez

Jabez was born in the tribe of Judah. He was born in a blessed family. So Jabez was born into a family of rulers. He was born in royalty. His forefather was blessed by Jacob in Genesis chapter 49. He was destined for greatness. His brothers were going to praise him. His descendants would always be rulers. He was blessed with the fruit of the ground.

V8 Judah, you are he whom your brothers shall praise

V10 the sceptre shall not depart from Judah

Genesis 49:8-11

Contrary to the prophecy, his mother gave him the name Jabez (he will cause pain). The name came about because of the pain the mother went through. It was based on circumstances in life not on God's word. Your outlook in life should be based on what God says, not the pain you go through. Pain is temporary, it will pass. *Weeping may endure for a night, but joy comes in the morning.*

Psalm 30:5

Jabez knew that he could change his circumstances. He refused to accept the status quo. He knew that he had been born in a blessed tribe called the tribe of Judah. He made up his mind for victory. He told himself that, "I can do all things through Christ who strengthens.

Philippians 4:13

He asked God to change his story. He asked God to enlarge his territory. Jabez knew that God was his strength, fortress, deliverer, shield and stronghold. He understood that with God on his side he would never go wrong.

God granted his request. He became honourable than his brothers. He was restored as a leader. He lived to enjoy wine, grapes, milk, honey and yoghurt. This was the life that had been prophesied years before to Judah his forefather. He lived a life of abundance and became more honourable than his brothers. This was because Jabez was willing to extend his boundaries.

Do not accept the status quo as permanent. Ask the Lord to extend your boundaries. There is more that you can do with your life.

CHAPTER 8

UNLOCK MY POTENTIAL

You need someone to unlock your potential so as to possess your pleasant mountains. Just as you need a key to unlock a door so that you enter in to a room. You cannot enjoy treasure stored for us in a room as long as you do not have a key to unlock the door. God has assigned people who will come into your lives at crucial stages to unlock your destiny. Such people do not come to stay in your life. They simply help you to get to the next stage of your lives and they walk out of your life. They enable you to possess your pleasant mountains.

Some of the gifts that God has given you are still sealed on the inside. You need someone to introduce you to the world. We need people who will identify your gifts and use their influence to propel us into your destiny. People who are prepared to invest in you. These people will unlock your potential. These are people who are willing to connect you with people that they know.

You need people who see the unpolished diamond in you at a time when other people see mistakes, fear and failure. God has already prepared people who believe in your abilities when others have doubts. He has put the right people in your path who are ready to polish your diamond so that we can shine your jewel. These people will help you to become better and stronger.

God has already prepared people who will open doors for you. At every stage in your life God has put people in your path to take us to the next stage. These are people who unlock doors for you so that we reach your destiny. They come to add value to what you already have. They appear for that special purpose only. They do not come to stay in your life. They are not meant to walk with you to our destiny.

Ethiopian eunuch

The Lord wanted the Ethiopian official to have a good understanding about the messiah. He sent someone with the correct information. God sent Philip to go and explain the word of salvation to the Ethiopian official. Philip was sent to the exact location where the Ethiopian official was. God did not send Philip to go to the Ethiopian eunuch in Jerusalem but on his way home. God knows where to find us. He has already prepared a Philip for every stage of your life.

An angel of the Lord said to Philip, "Get ready and go south to the road that goes from Jerusalem to Gaza". So Philip got ready and went. Now an Ethiopian eunuch was on his way home. He had been to Jerusalem to worship God and was going back home in his carriage. As he rode along, he was reading from the book of the prophet Isaiah. The Holy Spirit said to Philip, "Go over to that carriage and stay close to it". Philip ran over and he heard him from the book of the prophet Isaiah. He asked him, "Do you understand what you are reading?

Acts 8:26-30

After explaining the scripture to the Ethiopian official Philip was taken away. Philip was sent with the message of salvation to the official. Once he had fulfilled his mission he was taken away. These people only come to unlock doors for you. You enter through the door that they open for you to greatness then God takes them away. They are not sent to remain in your life.

"When they came up out of the water, the Spirit of the Lord took Philip away. The official did not see him again, but continued on his way, full of joy".

Acts 8:39

Joseph

Potiphar's wife lied that Joseph had tried to rape her. As a result Joseph was put in prison in Egypt. It looked like he would not fulfil his destiny. But God had raised a man to introduce Joseph to Pharaoh. This man was the chief butler. Here was a man who met Pharaoh on a daily basis. The chief butler remembered Joseph when pharaoh had a dream which required interpretation. He remembered that Joseph had interpreted their correctly. He recommended Joseph to pharaoh as a person who was able to give the correct interpretation to his dream. Pharaoh ordered that Joseph be released from the prison. Joseph interpreted Pharaoh's dream. Pharaoh was happy and he promoted Joseph to oversee the Food Department. The chief butler was instrumental in opening the door to Joseph's destiny.

Then the chief butler spoke to Pharaoh, saying:" I remember my faults this day. When Pharaoh was angry with his servants, and put me in custody in the house of the captain of the guard, both me and the chief baker, we each had a dream in one night, he and I each of us dreamed according to the interpretation of his own dream. Now there was a young Hebrew man with us there, a servant of the captain of the guard. And we told him, and he interpreted our dreams for us, to each man he interpreted according to his own dream. And it came to pass, just as he interpreted for us, so it happened. He restored me to my office, and he hanged him. The Pharaoh sent and called Joseph and they brought him quickly out of the dungeon".

Exodus 41:9-14

Saul

In order for Saul to walk in to his destiny he needed someone to pray for him to regain his sight. To be effective in the ministry he needed the Holy Spirit. God sent Ananias to pray for him. God knew where to find him. God gave Ananias Paul's exact location. God had already raised Ananias in Damascus where Saul would need help. God raises people to unlock your gifts ahead of time. He raises people in your locality.

Now there was a certain disciple at Damascus named Ananias; and to him the Lord said in a vision, "Ananias". And he said, "Here I am Lord". So the Lord said to him, "arise and go to the street called Straight, and inquire at the house of Judas for one called Saul of Tarsus, for behold he is praying: and in a vision he has seen a man named Ananias coming in and putting his hands on him, so that he might receive his sight"

Acts 9:9-11

Saul needed someone who was fully convinced that God had deposited great things in him. People doubted him because of his past. Again the Lord introduced another person to introduce Saul to the believers at Jerusalem. God sent a man called Barnabas. Barnabas stepped in at the right time. Even though he knew that Saul's history, he had seen him preach powerfully at Damascus. He knew that Saul was a changed man. The believers at Jerusalem respected Barnabas. They listened to what Barnabas said about Saul. They respected and valued his opinion.

Saul was accepted due to the integrity of Barnabas not because of his gift. People accepted him because they respected the words of Barnabas. This is what Saul needed to join and be accepted by the brethren. Once he was accepted by the brethren he spoke boldly. His gift began to be manifested.

He was able to shine. The key to his acceptance and success at the Jerusalem headquarters was the input of Barnabas, the son of encouragement.

And when Saul had come to Jerusalem, he tried to join the disciples; but they were all afraid of him, and did not believe that he was a disciple. But Barnabas took him and brought him to the apostles. And he declared to them how he had seen the Lord on the road, and that he had spoken to him, and he had preached boldly at Damascus in the name of Jesus.

Acts 9:26-27

Barnabas also launched Saul into a great ministry. After Saul had left Jerusalem, he went to his hometown of Tarsus. Barnabas went to Tarsus to look for him. He was fully convinced that God had given him a great ministry not for Tarsus only but for the whole world. Barnabas was willing to give Saul an opportunity to grow in his gift.

Then Barnabas departed for Tarsus to seek Saul. And when he had found him, he brought him to Antioch. So it was that for a whole year they assembled with the church and taught many people. And the disciples were first called Christians in Antioch.

Acts 11:25-26

This partnership worked very well. They were able to teach many people. The results were quite visible. The lives of people changed. They lived like how Christ had lived. People gave them the name Christians. This all started with Barnabas identifying the gift that God gave Saul. He supported him and gave him the opportunity to grow and shine.

John Mark

When Barnabas went to Jerusalem he also identified another vessel for the Lord called John Mark. He saw the potential in him. He saw treasure hidden in the woods. John was a jewel which had to be polished. Barnabas brought him to Antioch so as to mentor him. He wanted to give the opportunity to grow. Barnabas was instrumental in unlocking John Mark's potential.

And Barnabas and Saul returned from Jerusalem when they had fulfilled their ministry, and they took with them John whose surname was Mark.

Acts 12:25

When Paul (Saul) and Barnabas were about to go on the second missionary journey they disagreed on whether they should take John Mark with them. They had taken him on the first missionary journey but John Mark did not finish the trip. Paul saw failure in John Mark. He saw someone who was unqualified for the task ahead because of past mistakes.

Barnabas saw potential in him. Paul failed to identify the treasure in the woods. Paul insisted that they should not take with them. But Barnabas saw the gift in him and how it was covered by the woods. Barnabas saw that Mark would become useful if he supported him. He chose to mentor him. He wanted to give John Mark the chance to shine. Barnabas took John Mark on another trip to his hometown of Cyprus.

But Barnabas was determined to take with them John called Mark. But Paul insisted that they should not take with them the one who had departed from them in Pamphylia, and had not gone with them to the work. And so Barnabas took Mark and sailed to Cyprus.

Acts 15:37-39

However after some time Paul saw the gift in John mark. He saw how useful he had become. His gift had blossomed now. He now wanted John Mark to be on his team. He had grown into a useful player. *Only Luke is with me. Get Mark and bring him with you, for he is useful to me for the ministry.*

2 Timothy 4:11

So when people do not appreciate us we should keep on good things. We should continue to have a good attitude. God shall send a Barnabas to launch us into greatness. Continue to use your gift in Tarsus, in Cyprus or Jerusalem because Barnabas is on the way. To extend our influence we need a Barnabas to launch us into greatness.

Elizabeth

Now Mary arose in those days and went into the hill country with haste, to a city of Judah, and entered the house of Zacharias and greeted Elizabeth. And it happened, when Elizabeth heard the greeting of Mary that the babe leaped in her womb; and Elizabeth was filled with the Holy Spirit.

Luke 1:39-41

God has designed people in your life who will make your dreams come alive. They will make the baby in your womb to leap for joy. God has lined up people who will ignite your dreams. At times all we need is a smile or a friendly greeting. At times we need people who will take time just to sit with us. God sent Mary to see Elizabeth at a time when she needed company. That visit changed her life. The baby in her womb leaped for joy. God has already lined up a Mary for your dream to come alive.

Jesus Christ

John was sent to announce the coming of the messiah to the world. He clearly told the people that he was not the one that the whole nation was waiting for. He told them that the messiah was already in their midst. He showed them the rightful candidate for the messiah. *The next day John saw Jesus coming toward him, and said, "Behold! The Lamb of God who takes away the sin of the world! This is He of whom I said, "After me comes a man who is preferred before me, for He was before me". I did not know him; but that He should be revealed to Israel, therefore I came baptizing with water. And John witness, saying, "I saw the spirit descending from heaven like dove, and He remained upon Him. "I did not know him, but He who sent to baptize with water said to me, "Upon whom you see the spirit descending, and remaining on Him, this is He who baptizes with the Holy Spirit". "And I have seen and testified that this is the son of God".*

John 1:29-34

Alek Wek

Alek Wek was born in the Sudan. She left her country of birth as a refugee. She arrived in London at a tender age of 14. Alek went on to become a super model even though she was dark skinned. This was during a period in time when dark skinned models were rare. They were unheard of in some areas. She succeeded even though she did not conform to the ideal model of that time. God had put greatness inside her. The Lord made people to see her as a special model. She was new and exotic to the fashion industry. She was unique, indeed an African Jewel.

As a young black girl in a foreign country, she therefore needed someone to unlock her jewel. A modelling scout discovered her at an outdoor market in Crystal Palace. Her life changed forever. Ralph Lauren also helped to unlock her potential. He booked her to open and close his catwalk show. This was an opportunity usually reserved for the big model of the moment. This opportunity unlocked her potential. Alek went on to become one of the most recognisable faces in the modelling world. She brought a different dimension to the modelling world.

As a result of this rare opportunity, Alek appeared in many music videos by renowned musicians like Tina Turner and Janet Jackson. She also appeared in a movie called Four Feathers as a Sudanese princess called Aquol. She also designed hand bags called Wek 1933. This jewel became an activist raising awareness about the situation in the Sudan and refugees worldwide. She was able to share her talents with the world.

Alek Wek inspired many black women across the globe. Her success helped change the way people see beauty, especially among black girls and women. Many black girls and women began to value their beautiful black skin. They could now see a black girl on the front cover of major magazines. Her success brought inspiration to many young girls all over the world. All it took was a scout at an outdoor market to unlock this jewel into the world. This modelling scout unlocked her potential which enabled her to possess her pleasant mountains. God has already put people in your life that will help unlock your destiny so that you can possess your pleasant mountains. You have not reached your destination yet. Your future is brighter. God has something big in your future. He has put someone in your path who has been assigned to introduce you to the world.

Do not focus on where you are right now. Sometimes the hardships that you go through in life are just the steps you have to take to reach your God given destiny. Alek left Sudan as a refugee. What she did not know at that time was that God was taking her to the fashion capitals of the world. It was only later that she was able to put the puzzle together in order to understand what God was doing. This shows that an unpleasant season can be used by the Lord as a step in your journey of possessing your pleasant mountains.

CHAPTER 9

EXCELLENCY TO POSSESS

Excellency refers to quality which is good and above ordinary standards. God has given you the ability that you are not ordinary. Every person born in this world is blessed with a specific gift at birth. Some are teachers, lawyers, scientists, sportsmen and sportswomen, politicians or business leaders. No-one was born a failure. God love you so much that no-one is created as a carbon copy of another. He has given you a spirit of Excellency so that you can possess your pleasant mountains.

Tabernacle artisans

Moses needed artisans for the building of the tabernacle. God raised two men and filled them with the spirit of Excellency. These two men were called Bezalel and Oholiab. God blessed Bezalel and Oholiab with the gift of wisdom, understanding and knowledge in all manner of workmanship. God raised these two for the noble job of building the tabernacle. God turned them into top designers. God gave them the spirit of Excellency to design the furniture for the tabernacle. They made tables, utensils, and garments of ministry, the anointing oil and sweet incense for the holy place.

"And the Lord spoke unto Moses, saying, See, I have called by name Bezalel the son of Uri, the son of Hur, of the tribe of Judah. And I have filled him with the spirit of God, in wisdom, in understanding, in knowledge, and in all manner of workmanship, to design artistic works, to work in gold, in silver, in bronze, in cutting jewels for the setting, in carving wood, and to work in all manner of workmanship. And I, indeed I, have appointed with him Oholiab the son of Ahisamach, of the tribe of Dan; and I have put wisdom in the hearts of all the gifted artisans, that they may make all that I have commanded you.

"the tabernacle of meeting, the ark of the Testimony and the mercy seat that is on it, and all the furniture of the tabernacle, the table and its utensils, the pure gold lampstand with all its utensils, the altar of incense, the altar of burnt offering with all its utensils, and the laver and its base,

The garments of ministry, holy garments for Aaron the priest and the garments of his sons, to minister as priests, and the anointing oil and sweet incense for the holy place. According to all that I have commanded you shall do".

Exodus 31:1-11

Hiram the Craftsman

God also gave a spirit of Excellency to Hiram. God raised Hiram for a special assignment. He was raised as a special bronze worker. God gave him the spirit of Excellency. When King Solomon was building the temple in Jerusalem God raised Hiram to cast the two pillars of bronze and the two capitals of cast bronze. He cast the pillars by the vestibule of the temple.

He called the two pillars Jachin and Boaz. He also made the bronze carts and the lavers, pots, the shovels and the bowls.

Now King Solomon sent and brought Hiram fro Tyre. He was the son of a widow from the tribe of Naphtali, and his father was a man of Tyre, a bronze worker; he was filled with wisdom and understanding and skill in working with all kinds of bronze work. So he came to King Solomon and did all his work.

1 King 7:13-14

Ahithophel

God also raised Ahithophel to give counsel to King David. He was full of the spirit of Excellency. God gave him wisdom for counsel. He was able to give good counsel to King David. *Now the advice of Ahithophel, which he gave in those days, was as if one had inquired at the oracle of God. So was all the advice of Ahithophel both with David and with Absalom.*

2 Samuel 16:23

Daniel

God blessed Daniel with the spirit of Excellency. He was gifted in all excellent wisdom, knowledge and understanding of languages. He could interpret dreams and writings. He could also interpret puzzles. The excellent spirit in Daniel also enabled him to understand the literature of the Chaldeans. Daniel was very successful because he had an excellent spirit. This spirit made him to be different from other people. The spirit of Excellency enabled him to possess his pleasant mountains. He was promoted by the king to be governor of the whole province of Babylon. He was also promoted to be in chief administrator of all wise men of Babylon. This spirit of Excellency also benefited Daniel's friends as they were also promoted.

Then this Daniel distinguished himself above the governors and satraps, because an excellent spirit was in him; because an excellent spirit was in him...

Daniel 6:3

Chenaniah

Chenaniah was in charge of music when the Levites carried the Ark of the Covenant from the house of Obed- Edom to Jerusalem. King David commanded the Levites to carry the Ark of the Covenant on their shoulders by its poles. As they carried the Ark they had to play music using various instruments. They would play the tambourines, stringed instruments, harps, cymbals. Some of the Levites would blow the trumpets. The instructor in charge of music was a skilful man called Chenaniah. God put in him the spirit of Excellency to play many instruments. This spirit of Excellency enabled him to play musical instruments with distinction. Excellency enabled him to possess his pleasant mountains. *Chenaniah, leader of the Levites, was instructor in charge of the music, because he was skilful.*

1 Chronicles 15:22

David

When the spirit of the Lord departed from King Saul a distressing spirit troubled him. To solve this challenge the king needed music for this spirit to depart from him. So they needed someone who could play music very well. The king's servant identified David as the right person. The spirit of Excellency made David to play musical instruments very well. He could play the harp very well. It also enabled him to be a mighty warrior and to be wise. *"Then one of the servants answered and said, "Look, I have seen a son of Jesse the Bethlehemite, who is skilful in playing, a mighty man of valour, a man of war, prudent in speech, a handsome person, and the Lord is with him".*

1 Samuel 16:18

Sin a barrier to Excellency

Righteousness exalts a nation, but sin is a reproach to any people.

Proverbs14:34

God promotes people who fear him. He exalts people who do not compromise with sin. A person, community, country is blessed if the fear of the Lord is among them. The fear of the Lord makes people to be wise. A person who fears the Lord is blessed with peace, joy, success and Excellency in everything that he/she does. You need to have the fear of the Lord in order to possess your pleasant mountains.

"Reuben, you are my first born, my might and the beginning of my strength, the Excellency of dignity and Excellency of power. Unstable as water, you shall not excel"

Genesis 49:3

Reuben was Jacob's first born. He was supposed to excel in power and dignity. As the first born he was supposed to become to be a leader. But his father declares that he was not going to excel and he would be unstable because of sexual sin. Many people who were supposed to become great are just ordinary people due to sexual sin. Jacob declares that Reuben would be unstable as water. He would be tossed around like waves. There is no proper foundation. Sexual sin is a cancer to greatness. This is God's life principle which we cannot change. Young people live a life of sexual purity so that you will be able to possess your pleasant mountains.

Reuben was supposed to get the birth right as the first born but he lost it due to sexual sin. The birth right was given to the sons of Joseph. Even the listing of genealogy changed because of sin. *"He was indeed the first born, but because he defiled his father's bed; his birth right was given to the sons of Joseph so that genealogy is not listed according to the birth right"*.

1 Chronicles 5:1-2

Sexual sin robs many people of what they were supposed to inherit from the Lord. God does not compromise with sexual sin. Put away all sexual filthiness from your life and God will take you places.

"This is the history of Jacob, Joseph…

Genesis 37:2

The history begins with Joseph who was born as the eleventh son. Joseph went on to feed and take care for all the sons of Jacob in Egypt. His two sons Ephraim and Manasseh also got inheritance in the Promised Land. Reuben also lost rulership to his younger brother Judah. Jesus Christ came as the Lion of the tribe of Judah not Reuben. Reuben lost both birth right and rulership due to sexual sin. He lost dignity and power as had prophesied by his father Jacob.

Many people today who were supposed to excel live a life of mediocrity because of sexual sin. Some gifted people suddenly found themselves performing below par due to sexual sin. Their performance went down because it is God's principle that sexual sin lowers Excellency. Sexual sin removes Excellency in a person, community or nation. Young people run away from sexual sin to maintain high levels of Excellency at school, sports and life in general. The world is waiting for what God put inside you. Protect yourself by taking the right decisions. You have a great future ahead of you if strive for a life of sexual purity.

CHAPTER 10

PREPARED TO POSSESS

We have to be prepared to possess our pleasant mountains. Preparation enables us to achieve excellent performance. One way of achieving excellent performance is through practice. Even though we are all born to succeed we have to perfect our skills. Excellence comes through repetition. We have to do same things regularly. Sports stars take time to practice, actors rehearse and learners study and soldiers have mock battles.

The great Greek philosopher said, *"We are what we repeatedly do"*. The excellence in a sports star comes out through repeated practice. An excellent learner takes time to study regularly to bring out the best out of her/her. David Beckham is well known as a soccer legend that specialised in free kicks. The adage *"bend it like Beckham"* was a result of long hours of practice on how to take free kicks. To succeed in life therefore calls for us to constantly improve to bring the jewel that God put in us.

All Armstrong said, *"Champions do not become champions when they win an event, but in hours, weeks, months, years they spend preparing for it"*. Champions take time to prepare for tournaments. They spend hours, days, weeks and many months to perfect their skills. Excellence comes out of a long time of preparation. Real champions prepare themselves to ready for the event.

Many people want the glamour and the spotlight but some do not realise the amount of time that one has to go through greatness. *"The refining pot is for silver and the furnace is for gold"* (Proverbs 17:3). One has to dig to get gold. It is a process to get gold out of the ground. Gold has to be burnt in a furnace to remove impurities so as to get pure gold. God is ready to prepare us for assignments that will come in our future. His preparation takes time. We learn from the situations that God takes us through.

Moses

God waited for Moses until he was 80 years to send him to deliver the children of Israel in Egypt. He could not send him without adequate preparation. God waited until it was the opportune time for Moses to get out of the shadows. He had been a deliver since birth. He tried to do it early in his life with disastrous results.

Now it came to pass in those days, when Moses was grown, that he went out to his brethren and looked at their burdens. So he looked this way and that way, and when he saw no-one, he killed the Egyptian and hid him in the sand. And when he went out a second day, behold, two Hebrew men were fighting, and he said to the one who did wrong, why are you striking your companion? Then he said, "Who made you a prince and a judge over us? Do you intend to kill me as you killed the Egyptian? When Pharaoh heard this matter, he sought to kill Moses. But Moses fled from the face of Pharaoh".

Exodus 2:1-15

Without adequate training Moses got himself into trouble. His brethren did not accept him as a deliverer. He used fleshly methods. It was not yet time for him to deliver his brethren. Pharaoh wanted to kill him. He had to run away and seek refuge. Facing the world without adequate preparation can lead to frustration, heartache and consequently death. He killed an Egyptian who was ill-treating an Israelite. When Pharaoh heard about what Moses had done. He wanted to kill him.

God prepared Joseph to save lives in a famine that was going to come. At first we see Joseph as daddy's love child. His father loved him more than his brothers. He made him a tunic of many colours. *Now Israel loved Jacob more than all his children, because he was the son of his old age. Also he made him a tunic of many colours.*

Genesis 37:3

His father did not know that he was doing was prophetic. This was a confirmation that Joseph was destined for greatness. He had a special assignment from God.

God showed Joseph that was going to be someone great through dreams. So he said to them, "Please hear this dream which I dreamed: there we were, binding sheaves in the field. Then behold, my sheaf arose and also stood upright; and indeed your sheaves stood around and bowed down to my sheaf."

Genesis 37:6-7

Later in his life Pharaoh clothed him in garments of fine linen and a gold chain around his neck. *Then Pharaoh took his signet ring off his hand put it on Joseph's hand; and he clothed him in garments of fine linen and put a gold chain around his neck.*

Genesis 41:42

One day he would become the governor of Egypt. And when the time came his dreams came to pass. *And Pharaoh said to Joseph, see, I have set you over all the land of Egyptian.*

Genesis 41:41

God took over and prepared Joseph to become a governor. It was a painful experience from the time his brothers hated him because of his dreams to the time he became governor of Egypt. This made them to hate him. One day his father sent him to check on his brothers who kept the flock. His brothers treated him harshly. They put him in an empty pit, ready to kill him. His brothers then sold him to the Ishmaelites who took him to Egypt.

In Egypt Joseph was bought by Potiphar who was a captain of the guard. Joseph worked in Potiphar's house as a slave. The Lord was with Joseph, and he was a successful man in the house of Potiphar. This shows that we have to strive for Excellency wherever we find ourselves. Like a flower we have to bloom wherever we are planted, in the tropical rainforest, desert or even in the cold tundra region.

However Potiphar's wife lied that Joseph tried to rape him. Joseph was put in prison. It was painful experience. It looked as if nothing would go on well for Joseph. But even in prison the Lord showed him favour. The keeper of the prison committed all prisoners to Joseph. He was given leadership duties in prison. It was God's plan to teach him to become a great leader in Egypt. God was preparing for greatness to fulfil the dreams.

In prison he continued to excel in his duties. One day he interpreted dreams for two prisoners accurately. This was God's way to connect him to his destiny. After two years Pharaoh had a dream. Joseph was called upon to interpret the king's dreams. When he interpreted the king's dreams accurately and with wisdom, the king promoted him to become governor. His gift opened doors for him.

A man's gift makes room for him Proverbs 18:16

God prepared Joseph for greatness. It was long and painful but Joseph learnt life lessons that propelled him towards his dream. He moved around Egypt preserving food for the famine that was coming. When the famine came, his father and brothers came to Egypt looking for grain. Joseph was able to look after his brethren as their leader. Finally Joseph came to live his dreams.

David

The Lion…the bear…the giant…greatness

David worked hard behind the scenes as a shepherd boy. It was at this time that he killed a bear and a lion that came to kill his father's sheep. When a predator came for the sheep, he would take his sling and stones to protect his flock. He was just being faithful in his duties. He was simply protecting his father's sheep, not knowing that he was preparing himself for greatness.

David took time to perfect his skill with the sling as a shepherd boy. He took hours, days, weeks, months and years perfecting his skill. When the time came to fight the national enemy, David was already a sharp shooter. He had become a national sniper. He was able to strike the enemy with the first strike. What a remarkable story. This was the fruit of the long hours of preparation.

One day he defeated the mighty Goliath and became great. Even the women composed a song about him. They sang about his achievements. He was compared to the king. David became an instant celebrity. He became known throughout the kingdom. He went on to become the king's son-in-law. His life changed dramatically. He rose from obscurity to prominence in a single day.

David did not become a champion the moment he defeated Goliath in the valley of Elah but when he spent time as a shepherd boy perfecting his God given abilities. He fought and killed the predators which came to kill the sheep, the lion and the bear. *And David said unto Saul, "They servant kept his father's sheep, and there came a lion, and a bear, and took a lamb out of stock: and I went after him, and smote him, and delivered it out of the mouth: and when he rose against me, I caught him by his beard, and smote, and slew".*

1 Samuel 17:34-35

He fought and defeated the bear and the lion but was still unknown. Then when he had perfected his gift God gave him the chance to fight the national enemy. He was not afraid because he knew that he was able to do it. Experience is the best teacher. God had given him the time to perfect his gift without pressure. He had perfected the skill away from the people, press, criticism, public scrutiny through practice when he was still a shepherd boy.

One day he became a champion. He won the contest. He killed Goliath of Gath, the giant. This was possible due to the long hours of preparation. He was brought by the commander to appear before the king. He was now in the VIP lounge. *"Then, as David returned from the slaughter of the Philistine, Abner took him and brought him before Saul [the king] with the head of the Philistine in his hand."*

1 Samuel 17:57

If David had met Goliath before he was ready it was going to be disastrous for the whole nation. Many people would have died. Israel was going to be servants to the Philistines as slaves. It is dangerous to face the world without preparation. A learner who sits for an examination without adequate preparation brings heartache to fellow learners, friends, teachers and the whole nation. A driver who sits behind the steering wheel without adequate preparation can cause accidents, heartache and loss of lives.

Importance of preparation

It is important to be well prepared first before facing the world. We prepare ourselves through education and experience. Adequate preparation is important as it saves lives. Preparation improves our level of confidence. Experience reduces chances of error. God also prepares us for the next level in our lives through experience. It is therefore important to learn from everything we go through. Preparation is an important ingredient in the process of possessing our pleasant mountains.

Captain Chesley Sullenberger

A story that shows the importance of adequate preparation is that of Captain Chesley Sullenberger. He was instrumental in the landing of US Airways flight 1549 on the Hudson River on 15 January 2009. Many people were surprised to learn that a plane had crash landed in the Hudson River in the United States of America. All the passengers and crew on board survived the crash landing. Many people thanked God for what had happened.

The captain of the plane was called Chesley Sullenberger. From an early age he built model planes. He is a glider pilot. Captain Chesley Sullenberger also has a flight certificate for airplanes and glides. He could fly airplanes with or without engines. He has had over 40 years of flight experience. Captain Chesley spent time preparing himself to fly either a plane with or without engines.

His education and experience helped him to guide the crash landing of flight 1549 into the Hudson River without any loss of lives. His experience as a glider pilot helped him to land a plane with an engine that was malfunctioning. He was a well-educated and highly experienced captain. God used someone who had taken time to prepare himself to save lives. He had prepared himself through education and experience. Education and experience enabled him to possess his pleasant mountains.

#Flight 1549

On 15 January 2009, US Airways flight 1549 hit a large flock of Canada Geese upon take off from LaGuardia Airport, disabling both engines of the plane. The plane was carrying 155 passengers and crew on board. Using his experience, Captain Sullenberger quickly decided to have an emergency landing in the waters of the Hudson River so as to save lives. The emergency landing was successful. All passengers and crew members survived.

Speaking with news anchor Katie Couric on CBS News show called 60 minutes, Captain Sullenberger said, *"One way of looking at this might be that for 42 years, I've been making small regular deposits in this bank of experience, education and training. And on January 15 the balance was sufficient so that I could make a very large withdrawal"*. The story about the emergency landing of flight 1549 on the Hudson River in the USA shows the importance of adequate preparation. Over time Captain Sullenberger had been properly trained and prepared through experience. He had over 20 000 hours of flying time. His wealth of experience helped to save many lives. He became a world champion. He did not become a champion when he successfully landed flight 1549 on the Hudson River but over 40 years of learning and practice.

This shows that there is no substitute for adequate preparation. Every person needs time to fine tune God given abilities. We fine tune our God given abilities in schools, colleges and practical experience. What we go through is instrumental in preparing us for the grand stage. We get life lessons from both good and bad experiences that we go through. Captain Sullenberger was able to inspire many people today. He was able to do the unthinkable. He crash landed a plane in a river!

Stephen Cook

Another example which shows the importance of adequate preparation is Stephen Cook. Stephen Cook is a cricketer who was able to possess his pleasant mountains. Stephen is a South African cricketer who made his Test cricket debut at age 33. This could be seen as a late entry into Test cricket because he was now above 30 years of age. Some people would have given up the prospect of playing for your national team if they have not been called up by that age.

However Stephen always believed that his chance would come. He was prepared for Test cricket through playing first class cricket. By the time he got the chance to play his first match for the Proteas he was ready to excel. His experience showed as he went on to score a maiden Test century. It is considered a notable achievement for a cricketer to score a 100 runs or more on Test match debut. Stephen scored 125 runs on his Test cricket debut on the 22nd of January 2016 against England at Super sport Park in Centurion (South Africa). What an achievement! He became the 6th South African to do so in cricket history.

He was able to do it because of the experience he had gained in first class cricket. Stephen held the first class highest record of 390 runs from 648 balls. So when he finally got the chance to play Test cricket he was ready to shine. Indeed he was able to possess his pleasant mountains. He joined the elite club of cricketers who have achieved a similar feet in world cricket. Adequate preparation made it possible for him to possess his pleasant mountains.

CHAPTER 11

INNOVATION TO POSSESS

According to Merriam-Webster dictionary innovation refers to the act or process of introducing new ideas, devices or methods. Our God is an inventor. He has blessed his children with some innovative ideas, devices and methods. He has given you the ability to come up with clever devices, bright ideas to solve all the challenges facing the world today. Innovation in a believer is a supernatural birth right. Innovation enables believers to possess their pleasant mountains.

God gave the sons of Joseph the mountain of Ephraim in the land of Canaan. These mountains were occupied by Canaanites who had iron chariots. The sons of Joseph were afraid of these iron chariots. All they had to do what to come up with new and better weapons than what the Canaanites had. They had been empowered to come up with new innovations. God had given them innovative ideas. These ideas would enable the children of Joseph to drive out the Canaanites, Perizzites and the giants out of their pleasant mountains.

How would this be possible if God had not empowered them to invent better weapons to enable them to drive out the Canaanites? The sons of Joseph did not have this revelation. They could not see the beauty of their portion. Their portion was inhabited by Canaanites with chariots of iron. The children of Joseph had to overcome this challenge in order to possess their inheritance. God's children have to come up with innovations in order to live their lives victoriously.

The children of Joseph needed a revelation that God had given them the ability to invent new devices of war. They failed to come out with their own new weapons of war because they focused on iron chariots. This limited their ability to invent new machines of war. Fear of the chariots of iron limited their ability to come out with better weapons. God had given them the ability to invent great weapons to drive out the Canaanites so as to possess our pleasant mountains.

Engines of War

Uzziah became king at the age of 16. Although he was a young king, he had inventors who enabled him to have a well-equipped army. God gave Uzziah the ability to invent machines of war. The new invention enabled the king's army to be able to hurl large stones at the opposing armies. This invention enabled the army to have the latest technology of military hardware of the day. This enabled the young king to be able to defend the city of Jerusalem. These machines were put on the corners and towers in Jerusalem.

In Jerusalem he made machines of war invented by skilful men to be put on the towers and on the [corner] battlements for the purpose of shooting arrows and large stones.

2 Chronicles 26:15

80

Uzziah had them well armed with shields, spears, helmets, armour, bows, and slingshots. He also installed the latest in military technology on the towers and corners of Jerusalem for shooting arrows and hurling stones.

2 Chronicles 26:15

Other inspired inventors

In the beginning before there were universities and business schools God gave people business ideas through divine revelation. There are people in the scripture who ventured into projects where no other people had ventured before. The first person to venture into business was Adam's son called Cain. He ventured into town planning and architecture. He built a city called Enoch City. This was a unique project and unheard of in those days. He built a city, not just a single building. *And Cain knew his wife, and she conceived and bore Enoch. And he built a city, and called the name of the city after the name of his son-Enoch.*

Genesis 4:17

The second one was Jabal, who was a son of a man called Lamech. He ventured into animal husbandry. He was able to supply meat to other people as well. He did not copy Cain's business idea. He was inspired to do something different. He ventured into animal husbandry. He became the father of the meat industry. *And Adah bore Jabal. He was the father of those who dwell in tents and have livestock.*

Genesis 4:20

His brother was called Jubal. Jubal did not copy Jabal's business idea. He ventured into the music industry. He became the master of the harp and the flute. He was inspired of the Lord to go into this industry. This shows that God has prepared us for something unique and special. *His brother's name was Jubal. He was the father of all those who play the harp and flute.*

Genesis 4:21

King David

God also gave King David the ability to come up with instruments of music. King David was a worshipper. In order to worship well, God gave him the ability to invent musical instruments. King David was able to do it through the inspiration of the Holy Spirit. God still want His children to invent new musical instruments.

And the priests attended to their services; the Levites also with instruments of the music of the Lord which King David had made to praise the Lord, saying, "For His mercy endures forever…"

2 Chronicles 7:6

Tubal-Cain

The other inventor was called Tubal-Cain. The Lord gave him a different business idea from the one He gave to his bothers. He became an instructor of craftsman in bronze and iron. He was inspired to venture into the metal industry. He became the father of artisans. He designed decorative items in bronze and iron. He trained artisans to work in bronze and iron at his college called "Tubal-Cain University of Technology". *And as for Zillah, she also bore Tubal-Cain, an instructor of every craftsman in bronze and iron.*

Genesis 4:22

Joseph

Many people have died due to starvation caused by droughts. Changes in the weather patterns throughout the world have led to a reduction in the amount of grain harvested even in the world's major producing regions. A reduction in the amount of food produced can lead to food shortages. Food shortages are even more severe in food importing regions of the regions of the world.

God showed Pharaoh that a prolonged drought would come. He showed him what was going to take place in a dream. The famine would take seven years. This was not an ordinary drought. Pharaoh failed to interpret the dream. He was told by his chief butler about a Hebrew prisoner who would interpret his dreams.

Strategic food reserves

God gave Joseph an innovative idea of food preservation. This innovative idea came from Pharaoh's dream. The state was supposed to set aside one fifth of the harvest and reserve it for the future. These strategic food reserves would be kept in all Egyptian cities. The food reserves would be used to save lives during the seven famine years that were going to come.

"Let Pharaoh do this, and let him appoint officers over the land, to collect one-fifth of the produce of the land of Egypt in the seven plentiful years. And let them gather all the food of those good years that are coming, and store up grain under the authority of Pharaoh, and let them keep food in the cities. Then that food shall be as a reserve for the land for the seven years of famine which shall be in the land of Egypt, that the land may not perish during the famine.

Genesis 41:4-36

This innovation is still being used by many countries even today. Many lives have been saved over centuries because of this innovation. There was grain in Egypt when other countries had food shortages. *So all countries came to Joseph in Egypt to buy grain, because the famine was severe in all the lands.*

Genesis 41:57

Today the World Food Programme (WFP) uses this principle so to provide food relief during famine in many drought prone areas of the world.

Jacob and the new breed

"And it happened, at the time when the flocks conceived, that I lifted my eyes and saw in a dream, and behold, the rams which leaped upon the flocks were streaked, speckled, and gray-spotted. Then the angel of God spoke to me in a dream, saying, Jacob. And I said, here I am. And he said; Lift your eyes and see; all the rams which leap on the flocks are streaked, speckled and grey-spotted..."

Genesis 31:10-12

One day God gave Jacob an innovative idea in animal breeding. God showed him the new idea in a dream. Jacob used this dream to come up with a new way of animal breeding. He understood that God had given him a ground breaking idea that would change the world forever. Jacob followed his dream in obedience to what God had showed him. God gave him large flocks of speckled, spotted and brown sheep.

Jacob was shown male sheep leaping upon streaked, speckled and gray spotted ewes. He used the dream to come up with a formula of how to execute the dream and get the best results. He understood by revelation that God had given him a formula for a breed of sheep so as to prosper him. He was also able to determine the strength of the sheep that he was able to breed. *And it came to pass, whenever the stronger livestock conceived, that Jacob placed the rods before the eyes of the livestock in the gutters that they might conceive among the rods.*

Genesis 30:41

The Lord honoured everything that Jacob did in obedience to the instructions given in the dream. What limits us is what we see. The Lord showed us what He has planned to do for us in part. It is up to us to put in place all the invisible parts to a big jig saw puzzle. Success in life as Christians is determined by the level of revelation on what the Lord has given us.

It is important to act on our dreams, visions and aspirations. Our God is a God of new things. We should not be stuck to the old ways of doing things because He wants us to be innovative. God wants to bless us by coming up with new innovations in life. Even in unfair situations God has plans to bless us. He wants his children to be innovative.

He gave Jacob an innovative idea of sheep breeding through a dream.

And it happened, at the time when the flocks conceived, that I lifted my eyes and saw in a dream, and behold, the rams which leaped upon the flocks were streaked, speckled, and gray-spotted. Then the Angel of God spoke to me in a dream, saying, "Jacob". And I said, "Here I am". And He said, "Lift your eyes now and see, all the rams which leap on the flocks are streaked, speckled, and gray-spotted...

Genesis 31:10-12

Jacob acted on what he was shown in the dream. He understood that God had shown him the solution to his problems. He was abused by his uncle. His uncle had changed his wages ten times. God had a big plan for Jacob. This was a plan that was meant to promote him. This dream brought prosperity to him and his family. Jacob became rich due to this new idea in animal breeding. He was able to increase his flock. He became exceedingly prosperous and had large flocks. Jacob became exceedingly prosperous because of the new method of animal breeding.

Now Jacob took himself rods of green poplar and of almond and chestnut trees, peeled white strips in them, and exposed the white which was in the rods. And the rods which he had peeled, he set before the flocks in the gutters, in the watering troughs where the flocks came to drink, so that they should conceive when they came to drink. So the flocks conceived before the rods, and the flocks brought forth streaked, speckled and spotted".

Genesis 30:37-39

He took time to look for the poplar trees, Hazel and Chestnut trees. He worked hard on the new idea of animal breeding. With this new idea he was able to determine the type of offspring. That is the colour of the offspring and the strength of his breed. He was also able to identify his flock as it was now distinct and different from the other flocks. His cattle, goats and sheep were streaked, speckled and brown in colour. The innovative idea was to manipulate the mating stage. The offspring was determined by what they saw during the mating process. What they saw is what they conceived.

We were created to provide solutions to the world's problems. We are not ordinary but we are born to greatness. Young people, you were created and empowered to solve the world's problems. We are not created for drugs, alcohol and premarital sex. God is ready to intervene in your lives just as he did in Jacob's life. We have been blessed with many new things this world has not been such new variety of crops, books, new technology or fashion. Great things await us if we invite God in our lives.

Mary Hunter

Another trend setter is Mary Hunter. Her innovative idea contributed to improving the quality of big roasts. Mary enjoyed cooking for fellow Christians at her church. She thought that she was just an ordinary church woman. Little did she know that God had put greatness inside her? For a long time she continued serving at her church preparing big roasts enough for all church members. But there was always the challenge on how best to spread marinating juices on the inside of big roasts. She always wanted to improve her cooking. She wanted to possess her pleasant mountains.

One day God gave her an idea on how to marinate chicken better. God gave her an idea to come up with a stainless steel kitchen gadget called a marinating stick. This new invention allowed for the even spread of juices on the inside of big roasts she made for her fellow church members. Finally God gave her what she had always wanted. This innovation helped improve the quality of her cooking. Other churches also took on board the innovation. She later registered her patent and started selling her marinating stick. Many people bought the new marinating stick. It was a commercial miracle.

Mary told the New York Times that her invention was God inspired. She said, *"I don't have a cookbook. God gives me my own. Prayer is where*

I get 99% of my recipes". She acknowledges the Lord as the source of her inspiration. This shows us that the sky is the limit for the children of God. God did not create His children for mediocrity and to live life as second class citizens. God has put greatness on the inside of every person. There is an invention with your name on it. Pray to Him to reveal what He has put inside you. You are not an ordinary person. Just believe that he has enabled you to live a successful life. Your future is bright and safe in God's hands. He wants you to possess your pleasant mountains.

www.ingramcontent.com/pod-product-compliance
Ingram Content Group UK Ltd.
Pitfield, Milton Keynes, MK11 3LW, UK
UKHW041921310325
456929UK00001B/141